The TAROT SPREADS Yearbook

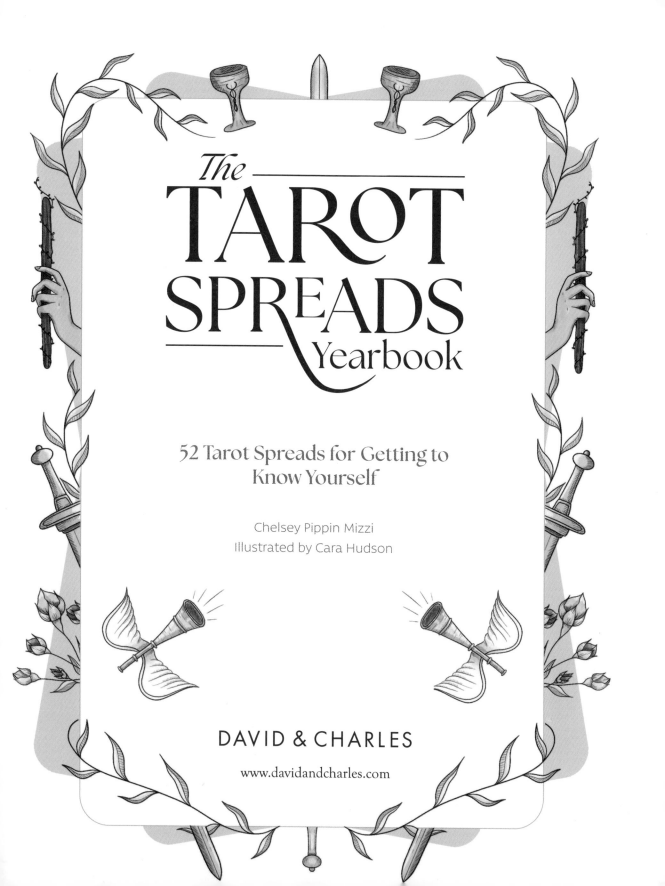

The
TAROT
SPREADS
Yearbook

52 Tarot Spreads for Getting to
Know Yourself

Chelsey Pippin Mizzi
Illustrated by Cara Hudson

DAVID & CHARLES

www.davidandcharles.com

Contents

A Year in Tarot..................................6

SEASON OF GROWTH 14

Growth in the Tarot 16
Intentions 18
Resources 20
Spirit...22
Mind..24
Career..26
Play 28
Friendship......................................30
Romance..32
Family...34
Conflict 36
Choice..38
Confidence.....................................40
Cycle of Growth.............................42
Reflections 44

SEASON OF SHADOW 46

Shadow in the Tarot.......................48
Intentions.......................................50
Resources.......................................52
Spirit..54
Mind...56
Career...58
Play 60
Friendship.......................................62
Romance...64
Family..66
Conflict...68
Choice...70
Confidence......................................72
Cycle of Shadow.............................74
Reflections 76

SEASON OF CHANGE 78

Change in the Tarot....................80

Intentions.............................82

Resources...........................84

Spirit...................................86

Mind...................................88

Career................................90

Play...................................92

Friendship...........................94

Romance.............................96

Family................................98

Conflict..............................100

Choice..............................102

Confidence.........................104

Cycle of Change...................106

Reflections.........................108

SEASON OF CARE 110

Care in the Tarot..................112

Intentions..........................114

Resources..........................116

Spirit................................118

Mind.................................120

Career..............................122

Play.................................124

Friendship..........................126

Romance...........................128

Family...............................130

Conflict.............................132

Choice..............................134

Confidence.........................136

Cycle of Care......................138

Reflections.........................140

About the Author..................142

Acknowledgements...............142

Index................................143

A Year in Tarot

This book is designed to guide you through a full year of weekly tarot spreads – but it's not date specific, so don't be afraid to start now. No matter where you're at in your calendar, it's always a good time to reconnect with yourself using the tarot as a tool to reflect on your life, your experiences, and your dreams. So, unpack a new deck or dust off an old one, and let this book be the map for your year ahead – your tarot journey starts today.

WHAT IS TAROT?

Tarot is a meaning-making system, and a meaning-making system is a tool for understanding your life – for observing the connections and patterns in your past, present, and future.

Humans have turned to meaning-making systems in the form of religion, folk tales, superstitions, and other traditions throughout history, as a means of creating order and, well, making meaning, in their lives. The tarot itself makes meaning through a series of 78 archetypal images, typically distilled into a deck of 78 cards that can then be shuffled and positioned into spreads that answer questions and prompt exploration.

Interpreting the tarot is a lifelong pursuit, and every reader approaches it differently. For some, the 78 cards of the deck are tools for channelling spirits and for predicting the future, for others, they are a tool for introspection. But across the board, tarot's primary function is to reveal what we can't immediately see, and to more deeply understand the meaning of your experiences and help you plan for your future.

TAROT AND YOU

Your approach to consulting the cards can be sacred and ritualistic, casual and conversational, or anything in between. You might read for other people, or you might read only for yourself. You could be a seasoned reader with years of experience, or you could have gotten a deck in your hands for the first time this morning.

However you read, this book is designed to help you deepen your tarot practice through weekly spreads, and reflect on your own life experiences, hopes, and dreams so that you have the tools and knowledge to manifest your best life.

Over the course of a year, the spreads in this book will bring your life into focus in challenging and illuminating ways. You'll make new connections, experience breakthroughs, change your mind about issues you thought long-solved, and ultimately walk away with a clearer sense of who you are, what you want, and how to care for yourself.

TAROT FOR ALL SEASONS

This book is divided into four seasons: growth, shadow, change, and care.

- *The Season of Growth provides spreads that will help you develop your relationships, grow your knowledge, advance in your career, and more.*

- *The Season of Shadow focuses on helping you confront areas of your life where you may feel shame, guiding you through spreads to uncover buried desires, deal with generational trauma, and challenge your own toxic traits.*

- *In the Season of Change, you'll find spreads to support you while you weather change, and also fight to make change - to your relationships, your job, your life, and your world.*

- *And finally, in the Season of Care, you'll find spreads to soothe you, and to help you soothe the important people in your life.*

While these seasons share some traits and themes with the four calendar seasons, don't feel you need to match a particular season to the time of year you're currently in. More than seasons of the Earth, these are seasons of the soul - and you can move through them at your own pace.

By following along with the soul seasons in this book, you'll develop a deeper relationship with the tarot and with yourself, and you'll start to notice patterns and connections in your life as you move through the year.

HOW TO USE THIS BOOK

This book is made up of 52 tarot spreads, one for every week of the year, and features prompts to help you explore your desires, fears, and needs. These spreads aren't designed to help you predict your future, but rather to reflect on your past, be more attentive to your present, and clarify your thoughts about the actions you want to take in your life going forward. So see this book as a resource for getting to know and love yourself better - as a gift for your soul.

Tarot knowledge

While you won't find a definitive guide to tarot card meanings within this book, that doesn't mean you can't come here as a tarot beginner. I welcome you to trust your intuition when reading the cards and not worry too much about getting the 'right' meaning. I wholeheartedly believe that tarot cards - and all divination techniques - are meant to engage our creativity and curiosity.

In some instances in this book, I've referenced the traditional meanings of a handful of cards, but if my words don't ring true for your unique relationship with a card, feel free to stick to what feels right for you.

Your tools

While I've written with tarot in mind, and use tarot cards as references throughout the book, you're welcome to use the spreads with whatever tool suits you best. The spreads will work perfectly well with oracle cards, runes, regular playing cards, or any other method.

Tarot journaling

I highly recommend keeping a journal to help you reflect on and record your journey through this year. You don't need a fancy grimoire to keep track of your thoughts as you move through the spreads - but if having a beautiful space to write in helps you feel more deeply connected to yourself, please take this as permission to get yourself one. Otherwise, a simple exercise notebook and biro are perfectly fine - as long as they give you space to spill your thoughts on to the page.

Throughout this book, I've offered up journaling prompts to help you integrate the lessons you learn from each spread and season into your daily life. Feel free to use these, but you should also feel encouraged to find your own journalling methods - you might prefer to sketch or write poetry in response to the cards you pulled, or you might like to follow the same journalling structure every time you pull cards in a spread.

Whenever I read tarot for myself, I like to do one page of freewriting about the topic of the spread or the question I'm asking before I shuffle my deck and pull cards. Then, once I've laid cards out in the spread, I like to journal about how each individual card answers the question I've asked the cards. See more about that in the sample reading later in this section of the book.

Types of spreads

Within each season, you'll find 13 kinds of spread. Each season opens with an intention spread, to help you centre yourself on the theme of the season, and set clear goals around what the season can mean for you. And you'll close each season with a reflection spread that will give you the opportunity to look back over all that you've encountered throughout the season, and where you can note what's changed, what's stayed the same, and how you want to carry the lessons of the season forward.

You'll also find the following topics in each season:

- *A resource spread to help you reflect on how the theme of the season affects your relationship with your things, your time, your money, and your energy.*
- *A spirit spread to help deepen your spiritual relationship by way of the season's theme. Note that spirituality can mean very different things to different people – but ultimately, your unique spirituality is nothing more or less than the way you feel most connected to your own soul.*
- *A mind spread, which gives you the opportunity to explore how your thought processes affect you during each season.*
- *A career spread to guide you through every season of your working life.*
- *A play spread to help you find the lighter side of each season.*
- *Friendship, romance, and family spreads will give you opportunities to reflect on your relationships through the lens of each season's theme.*

- *A conflict spread to aid you whenever you face discord.*
- *A choice spread to help you channel the magic of each season into your decision making.*
- *And a confidence spread to give you the boost you need in every area of your life.*

Note: You may come across a spread category in this book that you don't feel is relevant to your life – for example, the career spreads may not relate directly to you if you're retired, or you may simply not connect to one of the weekly spreads. If you find yourself looking at a spread you just can't connect to at any point in this book, feel free to replace it with your own original spread, or return to the intention spread at the beginning of each season and check back in with the cards you drew there instead.

Go at your own pace

You can move through the spreads over the course of one full year, but you don't need to worry about matching up to real seasons, or starting at a certain time of year. Whenever you decide to work with these spreads, trust that it's the right time.

You can also work through these spreads *ad hoc* as needed: seeking out the Season of Care's romance spread whenever you feel a hunch that your love life needs a little TLC, or turning to the Season of Shadow's confidence spread when you're struggling with low self-esteem. Remember that no matter what season you find yourself in, the lessons you learn can be applied throughout the year, whenever you need them most.

TAROT GLOSSARY

Here are a few key tarot terms you might find helpful to know as you move through this book:

Major Arcana

The collective term for the first 22 cards of the tarot, starting with the Fool (0) and ending with the World (XXI). The narrative that takes shape over the course of the Major Arcana, from Fool to World, is often referred to as 'The Fool's Journey'.

Minor Arcana

The collective term for the four suits of the tarot – Cups, Pentacles, Wands, and Swords. Here's a bit more about each suit:

- **Cups:** *This suit, which in some decks might be titled Vessels or Chalices, focuses on emotional experiences. The suit of Cups is associated with the element of Water, and typically shows up when there's inner work to be done rather than external action to be taken.*

- **Pentacles:** *Also known as the suit of Coins, Discs, and Wheels, the Pentacles represents work life and material investments. The suit is associated with the element of Earth. Like the Cups, this suit is less about external action and more about inner work. It encourages self-direction and determination.*

- **Wands:** *Depending on the deck you use, the Wands can also be called Staffs or Clubs. This suit is tied to spiritual and creative pursuits, and is associated with the element of Fire. The Wands is a suit of action, and is usually a sign that there's specific progress to make.*

- **Swords:** *Also known as Knives and Blades, the Swords is the suit of the mind - all its inner trappings and skills. Associated with the element of Air, the Swords are often indicators that a decision needs to be made.*

Court cards

Each suit features four court cards, typically titled the Page, the Knight, the Queen, and the King. These can represent people in your life, but also stages of expertise, with the Page indicating a beginner's mindset, and the King illustrating the height of wisdom. While the court cards, and many cards in the tarot, are illustrated by gendered imagery, their themes go deeper than surface level stereotypes, and I've endeavoured to be gender-neutral in my usage of them throughout this book.

Spread

A tarot spread is a method of laying out several tarot cards to line up with predetermined prompts. Maybe the most famous, and most simple, tarot spread is a past, present, future spread, where three cards are set out in a line. The first card corresponds to a past experience, the second card to a present issue affected by that past experience, and the third card offers advice for moving forward into the future, based on the context of the first two cards.

On the next page, you'll find a sample reading of a past, present, future spread to help prompt your own ideas for how to read cards in a sequence, and suggest where to look for connections to help pull a reading together.

SAMPLE READING

If you've been reading tarot for years and feel confident and at home in your personal approach to reading tarot spreads, feel free to move past this section and straight into the spreads. But if you're coming to this book as someone who is relatively new to tarot, or hoping to boost your reading confidence, here's an example of how I might read a spread for myself, which will hopefully give you some ideas about the ways you can make connections, build narrative, and get the most out of a spread.

Let's practice using a simple past, present, future spread. I'm coming to the cards because I want to reflect on the recent move I've just made, from England to France, and I need some guidance on where to focus my attention as I settle in. First, I do a short brain dump in my journal about what I'm hoping to get from this reading – I write about my experience of the move so far, how I'm feeling, where I'm confused or seeking answers, and what I hope I'll accomplish by pulling cards for myself. Then, I centre myself by taking a few deep breaths, tuning in to the feeling of my tarot deck in my hands, and my breath in my lungs. Finally, I draw my cards.

The first thing I pay attention to as I take in the cards is the feeling I get when I look at them. Which ones feel instinctively true before I even start to interpret them? Which ones validate me and which ones challenge me? Which ones surprise me, and which ones make me uncomfortable? I make any notes about what stands out to me in my journal, then I move on to consider each card, and the overall narrative of the spread.

For me, the Fool in the past position is absolutely spot on. I just took a big risk by moving countries. And the Eight of Wands for the present feels true too – I've got a lot of things in the air, and nothing has found ground yet – I have no permanent address, but I'm moving toward home. In the future position, the Knight of Pentacles is both comforting and challenging. I have a deep personal love for this card because to me, it offers a lesson about knowing my worth. But doing that in a new country amidst all of the various projects I'm working on is scary, and I know it will test me.

That, in and of itself, is a perfectly serviceable read. I'm going on a journey from risk to dealing with the flurry of good and bad consequences resulting from that risk, to feeling more grounded in myself.

But, by tuning into the finer details and letting my imagination start to work with what the cards might be telling me, I can go deeper. First, I make note of the elemental associations of the card in front of me. The Fool is an Air card, while the Eight of Wands is a Fire card, and the Knight is an Earth card. I can incorporate astrological details, too. I'm a Taurus, which is an Earth sign, which makes the Knight of Pentacles – an Earth card representing my future – particularly potent. It tells me that I'm going in a direction that really aligns with who I am at the core. That, along with my personal affinity for the card already, makes me feel really optimistic and empowered for what's coming next for me. Looking at the cards from an elemental perspective also highlights what's missing: water, or the emotional element. This prompts me to ask myself if I've been taking the time to check in on my emotional wellbeing during this change.

And the progressive direction of the elements in the sequence of cards – from Air to Fire to Earth, tells me that I'm going in the right direction if I want to settle and ground myself.

I look for patterns in the colours and visual cues of the cards, and pay attention to how that affects my overall perception of what the cards are telling me. In my deck, the Fool and the Knight of Pentacles are both framed by warm yellow, while the Eight of Wands has a backdrop of blue. I also notice that laid out in this sequence, the Fool and the Knight are facing away from each other. Visually, they look like bookends on either side of the Eight of Wands.

I walk away from the reading with this conclusion: I took a bold risk in making this move, and now, I have a busy but exciting road ahead of me. Ultimately, I want to find balance in my action-packed life. To do that, I have to remember the reason I made this change in the first place, and focus on grounding myself in the things that matter most to me – in what I value and what makes me feel valuable as I go forward into my new life.

It's a comforting reading, but one that ultimately reminds me that it's important to keep my focus even when it seems like a million plates are spinning (or eight Wands are flying). To help me integrate what I've learned and what I want to take away, I note down a few key actions that I can cross off my list and that will help me feel less devil-may-care Fool, and more grounded, focused Knight of Pentacles.

Season of

GROWTH

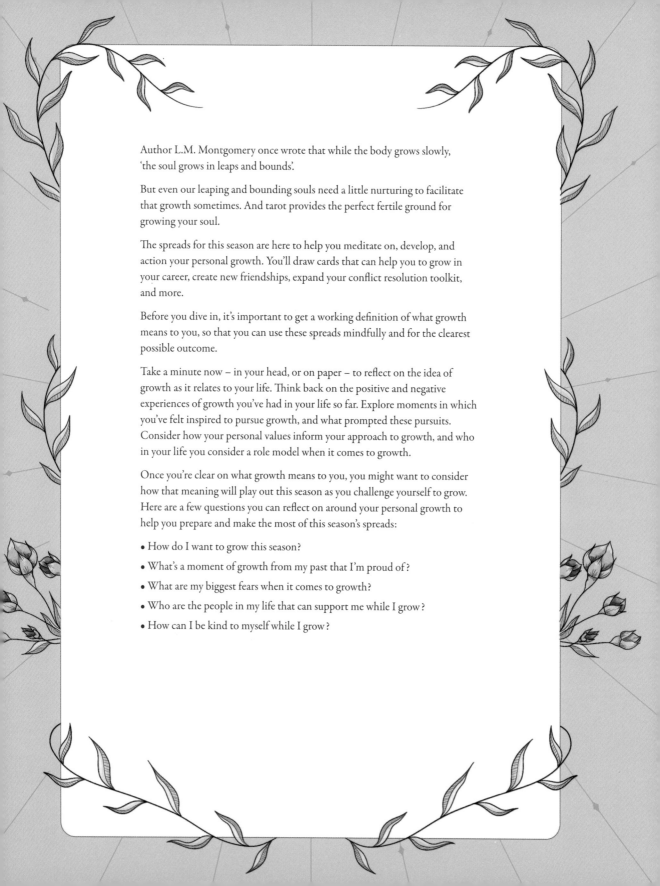

Author L.M. Montgomery once wrote that while the body grows slowly, 'the soul grows in leaps and bounds'.

But even our leaping and bounding souls need a little nurturing to facilitate that growth sometimes. And tarot provides the perfect fertile ground for growing your soul.

The spreads for this season are here to help you meditate on, develop, and action your personal growth. You'll draw cards that can help you to grow in your career, create new friendships, expand your conflict resolution toolkit, and more.

Before you dive in, it's important to get a working definition of what growth means to you, so that you can use these spreads mindfully and for the clearest possible outcome.

Take a minute now – in your head, or on paper – to reflect on the idea of growth as it relates to your life. Think back on the positive and negative experiences of growth you've had in your life so far. Explore moments in which you've felt inspired to pursue growth, and what prompted these pursuits. Consider how your personal values inform your approach to growth, and who in your life you consider a role model when it comes to growth.

Once you're clear on what growth means to you, you might want to consider how that meaning will play out this season as you challenge yourself to grow. Here are a few questions you can reflect on around your personal growth to help you prepare and make the most of this season's spreads:

• How do I want to grow this season?

• What's a moment of growth from my past that I'm proud of?

• What are my biggest fears when it comes to growth?

• Who are the people in my life that can support me while I grow?

• How can I be kind to myself while I grow?

Growth in the Tarot

The quintessential tarot card for growth is the Empress – a card that is steeped in symbols of fertility. While the Empress is often associated with motherhood and femininity, in this season you can think of the card more broadly, as a facilitator for growth. Allow the Empress to represent a safe and loving environment that encourages you to pursue growth in the areas you want and need it most.

Think of this card as a lush garden where you can safely plant seeds for growth and change, and make the space and time to water them. Think about who in your life approaches their own growth like the Empress. How can you emulate and learn from them?

The Season of Growth also has strong links to the entire tarot suit of Pentacles (which may also be called Coins, Disks, or Wheels depending on your deck). The Pentacles are associated with the element of Earth – from which life grows – and cards like the Seven of Pentacles and the Queen of Pentacles are directly related to facilitating and allowing time for growth.

In a number of illustrated versions of the Seven of Pentacles, we see a gardener paused in a moment of reflection as they survey their crop. I like to think that this card is a reminder that growth is not a race – that pause, reflection, and observation of your actions, your situation, and your attitude are crucial to keeping yourself nurtured and aligned to the path you set out to follow. The subtext of the card is this: You can't know if something needs adjustment or additional care if you don't take the time to look at it. And if you're not giving care where it's needed, your crop won't grow; it will just wither.

The Queen of Pentacles prioritises time, too. In lots of ways, this Queen is a visual twin to the Empress – both cards in many decks are depicted as pregnant figures perched on thrones in the midst of a meadow or forest. But unlike the Empress, the Queen of Pentacles has a certain tension in their physicality. There's a sense that this Queen is waiting for something.

While the Empress is fully relaxed, welcoming growth, how and as it comes, the Queen of Pentacles anticipates growth more intentionally, and considers the weight of their own investment in that growth. Both cards, ultimately, represent the idea that personal growth requires a fertile, nurturing atmosphere, but their approach to how to pursue that growth is in contrast.

In our lives, we sometimes may need to be more practical about our growth, like the Queen of Pentacles. At other times, we may need to take some space unapologetically and apply a come-what-may attitude, like the Empress.

Another Pentacle card that speaks specifically to growth is the Eight of Pentacles. The most common illustrated versions of this card feature a craftsperson practising their skill. Here is a simple and sweet reminder that growing takes work, practice, and happens in the in-between moments - growth is an action, not a destination.

As you start off this season, take some time to lay out the suit of Pentacles and the Empress. Reflect on what you feel each card says to you about growth, and how you'd like to apply that energy to your own life.

Reminder

Before you dive in to this season's spreads, remember: growth is never really delegated to one season. If we look to nature, every season plays its own part in nurturing growth. Winter is a time of rest that makes room for spring's fresh blooms, summer celebrates and basks in the lengthening of days, the fullness of the flowers. And autumn does the important work of shedding what's no longer necessary and makes a fertilizing mulch of dying leaves.

Take the opportunity this season to pay attention to how you grow, where you want to grow, and what kind of growth matters to you most, but don't let your growth end when the season does. Trust that the seeds you plant through reflecting on these spreads will continue to rise and bloom throughout the year, so long as you continue to nurture them.

INTENTIONS

When we want something to grow, we need to plant a seed. We need to water that seed, and we need to tend to it so it can blossom into a strong flower and bear meaningful fruit. This spread is designed to help you plant those seeds for your growth, and to prepare yourself for the growth journey ahead.

Your growth goals

You'll use this spread to map out the progress you hope to make during this Season of Growth. You'll identify your ambitions and intentions for growth, and take a moment to make sure you're aligned with yourself about what you want to see take place this season.

Before you begin

Before drawing cards, reflect back on the notes you made in response to the prompts at the start of this season. Also consider whether or not an intention ritual (like planting or eating a seed) might help empower you to connect more deeply to your intentions for growth.

When to use this spread

Use this spread at the start of your Season of Growth – or anytime you want to call in or prioritize growth throughout the year.

1. How I intend to grow this season
2. A misbelief I intend to release while I grow
3. How I intend to nurture myself while I grow

·◇·

RESOURCES

Whether it's your garden, your book collection, your bank balance, or your muscle mass, this spread is all about helping you grow a physical resource thoughtfully. It's a prime tool for when you want to do some serious manifesting.

Meaningful manifestation

Manifestation work is when you set clear intentions for a goal, and commit to channelling your energy toward it. Manifestation doesn't mean saying you want something and waiting for it to happen. It's about following through on a commitment to making your own desires real. These cards can help you do that, but remember that you'll have to commit to taking action if you want to see that growth.

So, whip out your cards and have a flip through. If you see a specific card that stands out to you, pull it out and place it in the first position of the spread (a physical resource I want to grow this season). If nothing really catches your eye or your heart, shuffle the deck and draw a card at random. Spend some time with this first card, asking yourself what resource it represents to you and why. Are you surprised by the resource this card is prompting you to think about, or has this been a long time coming?

Turn the message into action

Shuffle your deck and draw cards for positions two through four in the spread, and note down your impressions of what each card has to say to you. Once you feel you're clear on the message of the card, ask yourself these questions:

- What small action can I commit to taking toward this growth today?
- What action can I commit to taking toward this growth this week?
- What action can I commit to taking toward this growth this month?
- How will I reward myself for making even the smallest amount of progress toward this goal at the end of the season?

1. A physical resource I want to grow this season
2. Why this growth is important to me
3. What I need to do to facilitate this growth
4. How I can nourish myself whilst I grow

SPIRIT

Spiritual growth, on face value, can sound floaty and sweet. But anyone who's ever endeavoured to grow spiritually knows it's a seriously exhausting battle of wills against ourselves. But it's also so, so worth it in the end.

What are you growing?

Spirituality, of course, means different things to different people. But I think we can all agree that when it comes to spiritual growth, what we're looking for is a deeper connection to, and satisfaction in, the spiritual life we desire.

This spread can jumpstart a period of spiritual growth by offering you a challenge to help you bridge the gap between where you are now and the most spiritually satisfied version of yourself.

Before you begin

To prepare for this spread, put aside some time to connect to that spiritually advanced version of yourself by creating an environment your spirit thrives in.

Plan a few minutes of meditation, or some stream-of-consciousness journaling, or even a relaxing bath. Once you're feeling zen enough to explore your spiritual challenges, shuffle your cards while thinking about what inner peace feels like for you, and what stands in the way of you getting it.

Make prompts and reminders

Lay out the cards for this spread and journal thoughtfully about how each card can help you continue to build inroads with your most spiritually satisfied self. I recommend taking a picture of these cards and making it your phone background, to remind you of the challenge you've accepted, and what that challenge means for you.

1. A spiritual challenge I'm called to face

2. A benefit of accepting this challenge

3. A strength I have that can help me take this challenge on

4. A sacrifice I'll have to make as part of this challenge

MIND

This spread is here to help you reflect on, and action, growth within the context of your mind. In other words, this is a spread for learning.

What kind of learner are you?

Before you shuffle your cards and get started on this spread, take a minute to reflect on your relationship to learning in your life so far. Do you consider yourself a voracious learner, or a reticent one? A 'fast' learner or a 'slow' learner (but don't bring guilt into the equation here – trust whatever learning style or pace is right for you!).

Another question to consider, and one I often ask my clients, is how do you like to learn? Are you a conversation-haver? A documentary-viewer? A workshop-attender? A note-taker? Or are you the kind who likes to just get your hands dirty and give it go?

Where will learning take you?

Use the insights from these reflections to contextualize what the cards tell you as you draw them. Say, for example, you draw the Three of Swords to indicate how you learn. That may be an invitation to consider how unpleasant consequences can often turn out to be positive when they allow you to build your knowledge in the long term. The King of Pentacles drawn to represent where you want to grow knowledge could be a prompt to start learning about what it might look like to start your own business, or to be some kind of financial leader.

Be ready for anything!

Whatever cards you pull, think of this spread as research. You're gathering intel about how, why, and from where your knowledge grows. And when you come into your Season of Growth armed with awareness of how you learn and build knowledge, you'll be ready for whatever else the season has to throw at you.

2

3 **1** **4**

5

1. How I grow knowledge
2. Where I want to grow my knowledge
3. Where I want to share knowledge
4. Who or what can help me learn
5. How knowledge will help me this season

CAREER

If you're feeling like it's time to take the next step in your career, this spread can help you reflect on your present and future opportunities.

Focus on your work life

Whether you're looking for guidance on how to leave your job, how to advance at your current place of work, how to start your own business, or if you should take the leap and retrain entirely, you can look to the cards you pull in this spread for clarity and focus.

Some of my favourite questions to explore when I do career readings are these:

- What can these cards tell me about what I really value about work?
- Is short-term or long-term career growth more important to me right now?
- How could these cards help me set measurable goals for my career?

Consider the Pentacle suit

As you prepare to lay out cards for this spread, it's a good idea to reflect back on the suit of Pentacles, which we looked at when we started this season. Not only are the Pentacle cards related to Earth and growth, they're also related to occupation and professional stability. Cards like the Two of Pentacles can prompt you to consider your work-life balance, for example, while the Three of Pentacles is an opportunity to investigate how you feel about your professional collaborations and partnerships. Whether or not a Pentacle card comes up when you draw for the spread, now is the perfect time to look back over these cards and think about how their message can help you gain clarity and strength to pursue growth in your professional life.

Once you've drawn and reflected on the cards for this spread and the Pentacles as a whole, spend a week or so noting if and how these cards change the way you think about work, and what it means for your next steps.

Growth might not be change

Even if you don't have an active itch for change in your working life at the moment, it's worth checking in on where you're at with work this season, and seeing what comes up. From there, you could consider using your notes and observations from this spread as the basis of your next annual review, or to help you identify career growth opportunities you might not have otherwise pursued.

1. My current career situation
2. How my current situation is preparing me for bigger things
3. Where my career needs to go next
4. A skill I need to nurture so I can move ahead

PLAY

If you make only one goal for growth this season, I hope beyond anything that it's to grow your playful side. I'm a firm believer that human beings learn best through play, and we all need more of it.

The purpose of play

Play can enrich all areas of your life. A sense of play can keep your work life interesting and dynamic, your relationships fresh and filled with laughter, help you stay active, solve problems, and adjust to change. And of course, play is the key component in creative expression.

This spread is designed to help you brainstorm areas of your life where you can be more playful, and to identify the very real barriers to play you may have come up against. It can also help you plan to encourage more play in your life on a daily basis.

Define 'play' more flexibly

This spread can also help you to unlock a more flexible definition of play. I often find that my clients are held back by unhelpfully rigid ideas of what play is allowed to be. Play doesn't have to mean breaking loose and ignoring the rules all the time. After all, games are made of rules, but games are only successful if they use those rules to create a sense of play. So, while the idea of finding play by completely freeing yourself is seductive, the truth is that using prompts and instructions to

kick start your play is no bad thing, especially when you're new to it.

The tarot is a perfect way to use structure to facilitate play. Seventy-eight cards are brought together in a structured but flexible language that encourages interpretation and new connections. Facilitating play is a particularly potent message in cards like the Hanged One, the Page of Wands, and the Page of Cups. These three cards can be read as prompts to look afresh at what's in front of us. They're opportunities to play with what we have by looking at it in a new way, or with renewed attention.

The fun starts here...

In the spirit of facilitating play, why not set up a fun environment for yourself before you draw any cards? Turn on your favourite playlist, slip into some silly socks or your brightest jumper, pull out some colourful pens, and maybe even stickers and stamps, to decorate any notes you take as you work your way through the spread. And if you've got a particularly cheerful or playful tarot deck, there's no better time to whip it out than now.

1. Where I need more play this season
2. What's keeping me from playing more in this area?
3. What can I release to encourage play?
4. What can I embrace to encourage play?

GROWTH

FRIENDSHIP

This spread is all about growth in quality over quantity, and is intended to help you audit your friendships and figure out what you need more of to feel satisfied and supported.

Exploring friendship

The first card helps you reflect on the experiences you're having with your friends now, while the second and third cards will prompt you to look inward and work on yourself so you can be more open to the qualities you need in friendships.

Ahead of shuffling and drawing cards, take a moment to reflect on your experiences with friendship. Our friendships are often our deepest, most complex, and most rewarding relationships, so allow yourself this chance to explore what's going on in those friendships – and your broader relationship to the concept of friendship itself. In doing this, you're opening up an opportunity for the cards you pull to cut straight to the heart of what you need.

Before you draw the cards

Try taking 10 to 15 minutes to journal through the card prompts before you even pull a card, and see what feelings, fears, beliefs, and desires come up for you. When you do draw cards, compare their message to what you've written down. How do the cards fill in the gaps, challenge your beliefs, and support your needs?

Endings as well as beginnings

You might find yourself drawing cards that urge you to cut off a friendship that's no longer serving you – Death, the Six, Eight and Nine of Swords, the Eight of Cups, and the Hermit could all be indicators that it's time to move on. While ending friendships may not initially feel like growth, remember that pruning is an essential garden task to keep plants healthy. And we edit our creative work so it can be the best version of itself. If your spread tells a story about cutting back, you may want to consult this season's spiritual growth spread to help you strengthen yourself for the tough but crucial decision to leave a friendship behind.

The cards you pull may challenge you to open yourself up and be more honest and generous within your friendships – this is especially true if you find the Ace of Cups in your reading. Whatever cards you draw, you can use this spread to clarify what you need from your friendships, and what you have to offer. Through being more intentional in your friendships, you can grow them in both depth and number.

1. What I need more of in my friendships
2. A belief that's holding me back from getting more of what I need
3. One thing I can do to release this belief and get more of what I need from my friendships

ROMANCE

Whether you've got a fresh crush, are seeing someone new, or have been committed for years or even decades, feeling deeply connected to the person or people you're romantically involved with is the key to a successful love life.

Nurture intimacy

If attraction, whether physical or emotional, is the seed of love, then intimacy is the flower that flourishes under our care, nourishment, and attention to that sense of attraction. In other words, intimacy is the result of growth in our love lives.

Without intimacy, romance is all smoke and mirrors, so this spread is designed to help you reflect on your own relationship with intimacy, identify areas that you feel safe and confident to explore, and get clear on what you need from a partner, all so you can nurture that crucial ingredient for love to grow.

Cards to note

When it comes to exploring and growing love and intimacy using the tarot, you'd be smart to spend some time with the suits of Wands and Cups. Together, these suits are representations of passion and emotion – the key components when it comes to intimacy.

Cards like the Four of Wands and the Two of Cups can be very much about synergy in our intimate relationships, while the Four and Five of Cups, as well as the Five and Nine of Wands can nod at discord and loneliness when it comes to our intimate partnerships. Drawing any of these cards in your spread is not a guaranteed forecast for the status of your intimate relationships, but these cards can help you to run a health check on your current experiences, desires, and needs so that you can understand and meet them better.

Love yourself

Regardless of your current relationship status, when drawing cards for this spread, trust that a deeper understanding of your relationship and needs when it comes to intimacy will play a pivotal role in your romantic satisfaction. So don't just look at this spread as an opportunity to find a good love match or improve problem areas with a partner, try to see it as an act of self-love as well. Because when you know what you need and what you're ready for, you'll be able to feel more comfortable in moments of both romantic pursuit and pause.

1. How I feel about intimacy
2. How I'm ready to grow emotional intimacy with a partner
3. How I'm ready to grow physical intimacy with a partner
4. What I need from a partner/potential partner for our intimacy to grow

FAMILY

This simple spread is here for you if and when you feel ready to grow your family. It's a great resource for big moments of exciting but scary change in your family life, whether that's bringing new life into the world, committing to a partner, or welcoming someone new into a tight-knit social group.

What is family growth for you?

When we think about growing our family, we often think about marriages or children (or pets!), and this spread can definitely help you reflect on those big life decisions, but don't feel that if you're not itching to get hitched or have a little one that this spread isn't for you.

For many of us, growing our family is about building an unconditional support system – whether or not those supports are connected to us by blood or by law, or not. Found family is just as valid and important as more 'traditional' ties so please feel empowered to use this spread as a means of reflecting on who you bring into your inner circle.

The evolving family

Alongside using it for the more obvious family-centred decisions, you could use this spread to consult the cards when you're considering moving in with a friend, going into business with a sibling, parent, or spouse, or opening your home to foster children or at-risk people.

Remember, family is a complicated, ever-evolving social system, and we'll never have all the answers or be tied to all the perfect people. But when we self-reflect and empower ourselves to approach our closest ties with thoughtfulness, optimism, and compassion, then the opportunities for positive growth are beyond measure.

1. How will growing my family challenge me?
2. How will it benefit me?

CONFLICT

Conflict can often bring out the worst in us – our most defensive, stubborn, over-reactive selves. And that's more than understandable, because when we sense a threat, we go into hyper-protective mode. Angry or closed-off behaviours wall in the most vulnerable parts of ourselves, and that emotional fortress can make us feel safe.

Find growth in conflict

The problem is that growth needs the opposite of a walled-in fortress. It needs open air, light, and care. Growth happens when we allow our vulnerability to rise up through, and despite, our hardness.

That doesn't mean you have to be a doormat when it comes to conflicts in life, though. In fact, what it really means is that you deserve to find a way for the unpleasant reality of conflict to benefit you. You can do this by taking some time out to evaluate the conflict and how you can navigate a solution for your own highest good.

How the cards can help

Tarot, as it happens, is a great tool for grounding yourself in the face of conflict. The cards can help you take a much-needed breather, reflect on the situation, gain new perspectives, and find ways to grow through the challenge. That's why this spread is intended to help you quickly and directly take stock of a conflict and consider how – and why – you want to move forward toward a solution.

In the first two positions, you'll have a chance to examine the root of the conflict from your perspective, while the third card prompts you to reflect on how the current conflict is challenging you to grow. Drawing a card like the Ace of Pentacles here might encourage you to focus less on what you don't have, and more on what opportunities you do have. A card like the Devil might indicate it's time to get help for a damaging or compulsive habit or behaviour pattern that's impacting the conflict.

The fourth and fifth cards will help you to be clear on the elements of the conflict which are within your power to change – namely, your emotional response to the conflict and your next-step actions.

Be clear, adapt, and grow

By taking the time and space to become clear on how the conflict is playing out, and how you can adapt to benefit from it, you're creating opportunity for growth in adversity, and the cards are here to help you on that journey.

1. The conflict I'm facing
2. What I want out of this conflict
3. How the conflict is challenging me to grow
4. How my response to the conflict is stunting my growth
5. What I need to do to overcome and grow from this conflict

CHOICE

The tarot includes many cards that represent moments of choice in our lives. When I draw the Two of Swords, for example, I become hyperaware that I am at a crossroads, and that whatever next step I take will require me to grow into myself and toward a specific direction.

A card of choice

The Two of Swords traditionally, though not always, depicts a figure at a moment of stasis. The figure is blindfolded, seated with their back to the sea. Their arms are crossed over their chest and in each fist, the figure grips a sword held up toward the sky.

For me, this card represents all of the ways in which I weigh myself down and hold myself back in the face of change. The blindfold suggests I'm trying not to see my situation. The sea in the background is a metaphor for the possibilities I can't see. The crossed arms tell me I'm emotionally cut off from the idea of those possibilities. The swords in both hands tell me that I'm on the defensive. And the seated position tells me that while I may find myself at a crossroads, I currently have very little intention or motivation to choose a path and move.

Escape the indecision freeze

Often, when we're faced with choices, we can be overwhelmed and even blinded by the pressure of what may or may not be ahead. So we find ourselves, like the figure in the Two of Swords, frozen and ineffectual... unable to act. But this spread can help you to grow out of that freeze response and give you a chance to make choices more thoughtfully.

When you use this spread to consider how multiple outcomes can challenge and benefit you, you're doing the big task of removing that blindfold, and giving yourself a safe place to lay down your defensiveness and be vulnerable with your fears and expectations before rising to action. There's growth simply in allowing yourself that space, and there's even more coming when you make a compassionate, informed choice that centres your own personal growth.

1. The choice I'm facing
2. A path I can take
3. Another path I can take
4. How the first path will challenge me
5. How the first path will help me grow
6. How the second path will challenge me
7. How the second path can help me grow

CONFIDENCE

Probably the most recognizable cliché about confidence is that old adage 'fake it 'til you make it.' But more often than not in my life, that advice has caused more harm than help.

Don't fake it

Faking it 'til we make it forces us to shroud some part of ourselves and doesn't encourage us to investigate what success means, what kind of success we want, and how we're comfortable pursuing it. Real confidence is about shining light on who we are, and finding peace, pride, and strength in that illumination.

So, I prefer a different approach to confidence: don't fake it, instead, nurture it until it grows. You don't have to act like a 'success' until you magically are one. In fact, you can't do that. What you can do is understand your own needs and meet them – feed and water yourself, put yourself in the right conditions to grow, and over time, you will.

We see this lesson throughout the suit of Pentacles, but also in cards like the Six of Cups and the Star. Growth is not a hard, solid thing. It's soft, it's wet, it's earthy. It doesn't hold a rigid shape, it flows and it finds its way. Growth needs help, it needs support, kindness, and love. It needs confidence to prioritize these things.

Grow your confidence

Think of personal growth as the journey to gaining confidence, and of this spread as a way to celebrate that process. Before you draw your cards, ask yourself:

- What does confidence feel like to me?
- What kinds of situations and opportunities have helped me gain confidence in the past?
- What kind of experiences have knocked my confidence?
- Who in my life makes me feel confident, and how?

Close your eyes, take a deep breath and imagine yourself in a garden, surrounded by your favourite plants. Imagine yourself planting a seed from a pack marked 'confidence'. Think about what nutrients this special little seed might need. Open your eyes, and spend 30 seconds scribbling down whatever came to mind. Keep that knowledge of what your confidence needs to grow in your thoughts, then draw three cards to help you reflect on where you're confident, where you need to grow your confidence, and how you can affirm yourself now.

3

1 **2**

◇ — · ◇ · — ◇

1. Where I feel confident right now
2. Where I want to grow confidence
3. An affirmation that can build my confidence

Cycle of Growth

The wisest words I've ever read about growth come from the essayist Anaïs Nin, who wrote: 'We do not grow absolutely, chronologically. We grow sometimes in one dimension, and not in another; unevenly. We grow partially. We are relative. We are mature in one realm, childish in another. The past, present, and future mingle and pull us backward, forward, or fix us in the present. We are made up of layers, cells, constellations.'

Over the last 12 weeks, through the experience of diving deep into your own personal growth through these spreads, you'll probably have come to a conclusion about growth that's similar to Nin's. You'll have found growth easy and natural in some elements of your life, while in others, the seeds you hoped would bear fruit remain stubbornly closed up beneath the ground.

You'll probably have pulled cards for an area of your life you thought was already mature, or at least growing along just fine, only to find out that there's rot at the root - that you have to scorch the earth and start over somewhere. But don't be discouraged - the ability to admit you need to start over is proof of growth in itself.

What I love most about these words from Anaïs Nin is that they capture the cyclical, everchanging nature of growth. We are always getting ahead and behind at the same time. And the fact that growth is uneven, partial, relative is not a design flaw. It's a wonder. That something can bloom in imperfect, improbable conditions - that rot can be in one place and life can be simultaneously climbing toward the sky beside it... that our lives can be messes and works of art in the same breath, is the essence of being a human on this planet. Growth, I think, when it boils down to it, is about welcoming the unevenness, about moving with it instead of fighting against it. About celebrating the inches and not demanding the miles.

Nin says we are made up of layers, cells, and constellations. We're made too, I think, of seeds: full of potential, and waiting for their moment in the sun. They won't all get it at once; they won't all get it forever. But so long as we nurture them, they will grow, will live, will move us along in our lives.

Journal prompts

Take some time to meditate on Nin's words. Explore how her description of growth matches and deviates from your own experience of attending to your growth over the past weeks.

Ask yourself:

- *How do I feel about the idea that growth is not absolute or chronological?*
- *How has my understanding of my past and present experiences, and my future aspirations changed over this season? Do I count that change as growth?*
- *How has my understanding of - and compassion for - my own maturity and childishness deepened this season?*
- *What has the tarot, specifically, taught me about the real nature of growth this season?*

TAROT MANTRAS FOR GROWTH

Before you move on to the next season, I want you to think about how you can distil the most powerful takeaways from this season into a mantra that you can carry with you into the next. Use the tarot cards that have affected you most deeply over the season – or look back to the Empress and the Pentacles – to inform what you write.

If you're not sure what your mantra could be, feel free to take one of mine:

A growth mantra inspired by the Empress

I welcome abundant growth into my life. I am capable of, and committed to, creating an environment that is suitable for my own personal growth. I reject situations that stifle my growth.

A growth mantra inspired by the Ace of Pentacles

My accomplishments are direct results of my own commitment to personal growth. I am proud and I am deserving of what I have nurtured into being.

A growth mantra inspired by the Five of Pentacles

Prioritizing my growth can be challenging – even harrowing. But I trust that the hardships I face offer opportunities for me to understand and treat myself better.

A growth mantra inspired by the Eight of Pentacles

To grow, all I have to do is keep putting one foot in front of the other, and celebrate every small win as it comes.

Write your chosen mantra on a sticky note and put it somewhere you can see it – or practice copying it out at the start of daily journal sessions. Refer back to it whenever you feel stuck, or whenever you want to call growth into your life.

GROWTH

REFLECTIONS

Your last task this season, before you move on to the Season of Shadow, is to draw some final cards to reflect on all of your experiences over the past 12 weeks.

Summing up your growth

Through this spread, I hope you'll gain clarity, cement pride, and set goals that align with everything you've learned about what growth means to you this season.

Remember that this reflection spread is for you, so if you need to change the positions or add new ones to get the most out of your reflection time, I encourage you to do it. See this spread as a jumping off point to help you integrate the wisdom you've grown by taking the time to dive deep into your relationship with growth.

One more card...

Consider too, pulling an extra card that symbolizes your personal growth style - and keep this in mind whenever you face challenges to your growth.

1. How I've grown the most this season
2. The biggest lesson I've learned through growth
3. Where I want to continue to grow

Season of
SHADOW

Shadow work was popularized by the psychologist Carl Jung, who proposed that everyone has a 'shadow', but most people are not conscious of their own. That's because shadows are associated with darkness. Psychologically speaking, these are the parts of ourselves that we've been conditioned to believe should never see the light of day. Jung believed the only way to grow beyond our worst parts is to recognize that they exist. Once recognized, we have to accept them and, to some extent, embrace them.

It's not easy work to do, but to carry on growing, it's essential. This season's spreads will help you begin that work. If there's one thing I hope you'll take away from this season, it's that your shadow doesn't make you dysfunctional. In fact, working with your shadow in context is the only way to function. Because here's the truth: a shadow, in and of itself, is no bad thing. After all, on hot summer days we crave the cool relief of shade. But when we're already cold and wet, a shadow may no longer be helpful – sometimes you'll have to cast your shadow out, and other times you might find the shade a blessing. Some of the spreads you'll try over the coming months are about embracing shadow, some of them are about simply recognizing it, and some are about actively challenging it.

Before you begin, take time to become more aware of your own shadow. It's a slippery concept, so I recommend drawing a tarot card to represent the facet of it that you would like to tap into and work with. This will give you focus and clarity as you move through the spreads. With this card in mind you might also like to journal your way through the following questions:

- What are my physical and emotional reactions to this card?

- Am I comfortable with what this card says about me, and my shadow self?

- What is this card telling me about my shadow that I already know?

- What new information does this card give me about my shadow?

- How do I typically interact with my shadow, as represented by this card?

- How would I *like* to interact with my shadow, and how might this card help me?

Shadow in the Tarot

As a theme, the idea of shadow is potent throughout the Major Arcana, with each card revealing its own perspective on shade and its counterpart, light.

The Devil, as a card about vices, hang-ups, addictions, and behavioural issues is probably the most obvious Shadow card, and it's an important one to reflect on because it invites you to consider the ways you're attached to your shadow, and why. It's also a card that, simply for the fact that it exists in the tarot at all, acknowledges that our vices, hang-ups, addictions, and behavioural issues are part of our human experience. The Devil reminds us that shit happens, and so do shadows.

The Tower, which directly follows the Devil in the Major Arcana sequence, is a card about the consequences of both ignoring and casting a light on your shadow. The Tower tends to have two meanings: it's about epiphany, or it's about destruction. In either case, it's about things crashing down – and shadow work will do that. When you ignore your shadow, forces outside your control tear you down and you're ill-equipped to deal with it. When you acknowledge and embrace your shadow, something else happens - you tear down the walls that you built to hide within.

The Moon and the High Priestess look at shadow from a slightly different angle – bringing to light the strangeness, the depth, the subconscious, and natural power of the shadow on our lives. The visual motifs of the High Priestess suggest a perfect balance of light and shadow, and the wisdom that comes from studying your own shadow and light sides. The Moon, on the other hand, captures the experience of being out of your own depth... the strange, dream-like quality of what's going on outside your conscious experience. The card advises you to accept that there may be parts of yourself that you never understand.

Meanwhile, the Sun and Judgment both illustrate the brilliance that comes with casting a light on our shadow. Freedom, acceptance, integration - these can feel like they're a million miles away from the dark parts of us, but they're merely the flip side.

Shadow is present throughout the suits of the tarot, too - most strongly in the Swords. But the truth is, you'll find shadows wherever you look for them in the tarot. So as part of your preparation for this season, go through your deck and draw out the cards that scream Shadow loudest to you. Spend some time journaling on how these cards intersect with the one you drew to represent your shadow this season. Keep these learnings in mind as you work through the spreads.

Reminder

As you move through this season, I hope you'll come to the same conclusion about shadow that I have: the work we do to understand and embrace and challenge our shadow self is not inherently dark or light. It's not good or evil. It's just human.

Seeing and honouring the reality of your shadow is nothing more or less than an exercise in honouring your humanity and everything that that encompasses.

The tarot, as a visual system, is incredibly adept at capturing light and shadow in one image in a way words can't - so look to the tarot as a mirror this season. See yourself in every slant of light and dark and know your depth, your humanity, comes from the combination of those qualities.

INTENTIONS

Embracing and confronting your shadow are the twin pillars of shadow work – you need to do both. If all we ever try to do is root our shadow selves out, we lose self-awareness, increase self-destruction, and deny ourselves a deep, meaningful, accepting relationship with our souls.

Embrace your shadow

We're kicking off this season's Intentions spread by investigating just how you can go about embracing your darkness. And because the tarot loves a plot twist, you might be surprised by the cards that appear to help you embrace your shadow.

Keep your shadow in check

Once you've done the hard work of finding a way to embrace your shade, the next step is to figure out how you'll challenge it this season. Because even though we owe ourselves the essential kindness of identifying the ways in which our shadows help us in this life, we also have to make sure we understand how to keep that shadow in check, and turn its energy toward beneficial, instead of destructive, tendencies.

Make a care plan

Your final draw in this spread will help you to prioritize self-care this season. Shadow work is hard work, so you need and deserve the padding of a care plan to ferry you through the truth bombs you're preparing to face. Whatever card you draw here, think deeply about how it reveals the kind of support you'll need over the coming months.

1. How I can embrace my shadow this season
2. How I can challenge my shadow this season
3. How to take care of myself while I work through the Season of Shadow

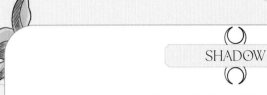

RESOURCES

Maybe the most famous of the Seven Deadly Sins, greed is a quality that our society is forever burying in shame, judgment, and punishment. But while greed may not be an attractive quality, it's also an undeniably human one.

Acknowledge your uglier side

The Season of Shadow offers an opportunity to acknowledge and accept the uglier sides of our humanity so that we can move forward. This spread is designed to help you do exactly that, by helping you become a bit more comfortable with your own greed. Because whether you like to admit it or not, you're greedy for something in this life.

Reframe your greed

Through this spread, you'll draw cards to help you identify the kinds of resources that trigger your 'greed', and then you'll move on to rethinking your relationship to these resources. The second position, which reframes your 'greed' is particularly important. Drawing a card like the Star or the Four of Swords here may reveal that your desire isn't greed at all – it's need. Need for care, rest, respite.

You might draw a tougher card, like the Six of Pentacles, which could suggest that you feel 'greedy' for a resource that has been denied to you in the past, or which you believe will balance out your life. Or you might draw the Lovers, a hint that your desire for a specific resource is overshadowing your other commitments and passions.

Find balance

The final position offers you a chance to balance out the shadow greed can cast – not by cancelling the greed from your life absolutely, but by challenging you to find ways to be just as generous as you are 'greedy'.

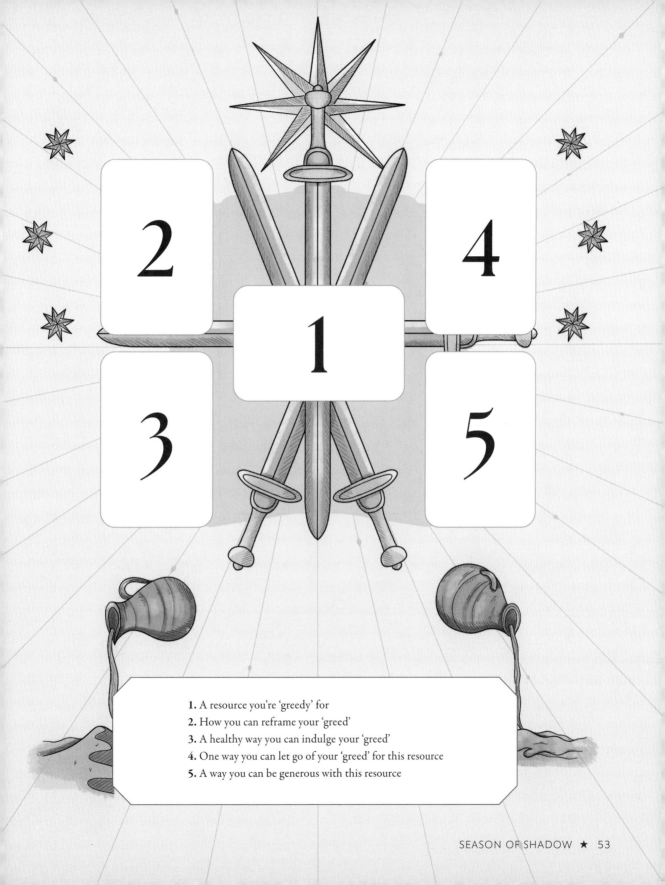

1. A resource you're 'greedy' for
2. How you can reframe your 'greed'
3. A healthy way you can indulge your 'greed'
4. One way you can let go of your 'greed' for this resource
5. A way you can be generous with this resource

SPIRIT

This spread is all about exploring the role of your shadow side when it comes to your spiritual wellness. Part of being in touch, and cultivating a relationship, with that part of you is about recognizing the light and the dark aspects that live there.

Connect with your shadow

You can use this spread to allow your shadow side to deepen your relationship and your understanding of your own spiritual journey.

Learn your lesson

The first three questions focus on helping you home in on a specific spiritual lesson your shadow side wants you to learn. The fourth question is more general, but no less important, and provides crucial context for the first three spread positions. Use this final card as an opportunity to add depth and connections to the first three cards in the spread.

Make room to explore

I recommend pairing this spread with a journaling session – though if it feels too tricky or troubling to put your thoughts about the cards you draw into words, consider doodling or collaging in response to the spread instead. The important thing is to give yourself room to explore, and work toward articulating the spiritual journey you're on.

Give yourself time and space to chew on the things you find as a result of drawing cards for this spread. Snap a picture of your cards, or leave them out on your desk, and come back to them throughout the week.

1. What spiritual lesson can my shadow side teach me this season?
2. Why is this lesson important for me?
3. What challenge might stand in the way of learning this lesson?
4. How does my shadow inform my spirituality?

MIND

Over the course of our lives, we've all developed problematic thought patterns. A lot of these developed early, as coping mechanisms that have only truly become adverse as we've moved into adulthood.

Find the root cause

Here's an example from my own life: I grew up in a military family, and moved around often. The internet as a means of staying connected with people didn't really come about until my early teens. As a kid, I developed a thought pattern that it was impossible to stay connected to people once I'd moved. At the time, this helped me let go of childhood friendships that ended over cross-country moves I couldn't control. It also (misguided as it was) helped me protect myself from getting attached to people I expected to lose as a result of moves – whether mine or theirs.

Cast a light

But just because this thought process helped (i.e., had positive consequences), that doesn't mean it was healthy. It wasn't until I was an adult (one who has now made two international moves of my own volition) that I started to understand how the belief that I was not allowed to hold onto long-term friendships cast a shadow over my whole understanding of the idea of friendship.

Believe in possibility

It wasn't that I couldn't hold onto friendships, it's just that I had to learn how – to believe it was possible, and that I was capable of it. I'm proud to say now that I have friends from around the world – relationships I may maintain imperfectly, but do maintain nonetheless.

Unknot the problem

Use this spread to examine your own problematic thought patterns – those that serve you in some ways but also cast a shadow over your sense of self, your agency, your capabilities. Whether your negative thought patterns are about money, body image, relationships, work, or something else, this spread can help you dig deep into the reason this thought pattern exists, why you cling to it, and the reasons you want to let it go.

1. A problematic thought pattern I'm experiencing

2, 3, & 4. The negative consequences of that thought pattern

5 & 6. The positive consequences of that thought pattern

7. How can I shed new light on this thought pattern?

CAREER

For many of us, our identity and our work are inextricable. This can be a beautiful thing because identifying with your work allows you to engage fully and passionately with your daily tasks.

Rebalance work and life

But when you identify too much with your work, it can create a pattern where negative experiences with work create a domino effect on your self-esteem, impacting how you see yourself in a broader sense.

This spread is here to help you rebalance positive and negative work experiences so that you can have a more compassionate approach to the way your work dovetails into your life and identity.

Define what you want

This spread invites you to first draw a card and reflect on what you want out of your career. As you explore how the first card illustrates your desires, think too about how these desires can be met in other ways beyond your work life. If you draw the Empress here, for example, your career goal may very much be rooted in the desire to run your own company, or at least to be confidently and successfully self-employed.

But the Empress can also tell you a lot about how you want to engage with the other aspects of your life – it's an opportunity to check in on how you're caring for and respecting your body, the dynamic that you bring to community and intimate relationships, or it could be pointing out someone in your life who exudes Empress energy that you could go to for support, guidance, and mentorship in your career.

Integrate your experiences

The next card can give context as to why you're not where you want to be on your career journey. Drawing Temperance, for example, may suggest you're well on your way as long as you focus on the work in front of you, while the Five of Swords could indicate that there's some discord among your team that's creating tension and blockages.

Cards three and four can help you contextualize and balance your past experiences at work. Once you've reflected on them, card five can help you integrate your positive and negative work history indicating a path forward that combines light and shadow to help you on your way.

1. What I want out of my career
2. What's blocking me
3. A negative career experience from my past
4. A positive career experience from my past
5. How I can combine these experiences for my advantage

SHADOW

PLAY

We often relegate our 'naughty' or 'cheeky' sides into shadow –
because we want to be good, we want to fit in, we want to get things
right, it can be tempting to see the spicier aspects of ourselves as
things we need to hide, tamp down, or keep to ourselves.

Push boundaries through play

This is a spread about loosening up and letting your freaky flag fly a little bit. It's about recognizing and honouring the areas in which you want to - but may be afraid to - have more fun.

In the spirit of fun, this is a great spread to use with a deck that pushes boundaries in some way. The Thoth's intense colours and visions, the Pulp Tarot's big personality, or the Desert Illuminations deck's trippy illustrations could all be great choices here.

Indulge yourself

Once you've picked a deck that makes you feel as bold as you hope this spread will encourage you to feel, draw three cards according to the spread positions listed. The first card will help you identify an area where you can be more indulgent to your desire for play, even if it's non-traditional or unexpected.

The second card gives you room to explore the reasons why you may feel pressure to cover up this desire, or even feel shame around the impulse to play.

The final card is a rallying cry to tease your playful side out of the shadow and into the light.

1. How my shadow self can help me be more playful
2. Why I'm burying my shadow self's playful side
3. What I can do to invite my shadow out to play

FRIENDSHIP

Navigating toxic relationships is a painful, but deeply human experience we all encounter in our lives. We've all had a toxic friend before... and chances are that we've all been one, too.

Approach with curiosity

Because this is the Season of Shadow, and because the tarot is such a handy tool for helping cast light on those icky corners of our lives, I encourage you to approach this spread with curiosity – about your relationships and yourself – because not only will the cards here help you figure out how to deal with toxic people in your life, they'll also prompt you to examine your own toxic traits.

It's important to do both – to reflect on the toxic things that happen to you, and the toxic things you do – because exploring these things in tandem will help you to be compassionate and fair to yourself and others. To re-examine the things that have happened to you, and the things you've done, in a new way.

Examine the grey areas

This isn't a spread that inherently requires you to forgive anyone, or take the blame, but it is a spread that, when laid out thoughtfully, can allow you a safe space to examine the grey areas in your toxic friendships and decide on a better way for you to move forward – whether you've been the victim, perpetrator, or both.

Capture your experience

Instead of drawing the first card at random, I suggest looking at your deck and drawing a card that matches your feelings about a particularly toxic situation, or toxic friendship pattern you've observed in your life.

Empower yourself

Once you've reflected on the card that illustrates your toxic friendship experiences, lay out the remaining cards as normal. Take time to think about how they shine a light on the shame and hurt of toxic friendships by giving insight into your behaviour, your choices, and finally offering some empowering advice for moving beyond toxic friendship experiences in the future.

1. What toxic friendship looks like to me
2. How I contribute to toxicity in my friendships
3. How I deal with toxicity in my friendships
4. How I can unknot toxic patterns in my friendships

ROMANCE

In romantic relationships, it can be easy to forget that identifying and asking for what you want are valid things to do. There can be a sense of having to take whatever's offered – that the only way to get your partner's consent is for whatever they give you to be their idea, and not yours. But that's simply not true.

Develop transparency

Having wants and needs in a relationship beyond what a partner is offering you is not shameful or embarrassing, and you are allowed to express them.

Of course, your partner is allowed to decline just as much as you are allowed to ask, but the conversation is always worth having, because it has the power to elevate you and your partner to a higher level of transparency, honesty, and understanding. It's that conversation - that level of transparency, honesty, and understanding with your partner, but also with yourself - that this spread can help you prepare for.

Reach below your surface

The first step to asking for what you want is knowing what you want. The first card you draw for this spread is designed to help you reach below your own surface and draw out desires you may have been burying, but this spread also fits nicely with this season's spread for Play, and it's worth reflecting back on what you learned through that spread while you pull cards for this one.

Unbury your desires

Bear in mind that this buried desire may be related to your physical relationship, or the next step on your imagined relationship trajectory (i.e. moving in, getting engaged, etc) but by no means has to be. Drawing the Star or the Four of Swords in this position would probably indicate that the desire you have is actually for space and distance from your partner - less we-time and more me-time. But that can be just as hard and scary to admit as suggesting a spicy addition to your sex life, or starting a conversation about parenthood.

Start a conversation

After you've done the big work of shining a light on your hidden wants and needs, the cards that follow will help you better understand and own the buried desires in your relationships. By sitting with and considering these cards and what they mean to you, you can give yourself a solid framework for how to then express your wants and needs to your partner.

1. Something I'm afraid to admit I want from my partner/future partner
2. Why I'm afraid to admit this desire
3. How I can grow more comfortable with this desire
4. Why it's important and empowering for me to own this desire

FAMILY

No one is shaped by their own experiences alone. The experiences of your family – blood or found – can have profound effects on how you see and navigate the world. That means that some elements of you live in the shadows, not because you put them there, but because they were already there when you came into this world.

Unpack your history

Through this spread, you can start to unpack those things that cast a shadow over your life experience before you even had a life to live. From there, you can move out of the darkness of the unknown, and into the light of understanding so that you can take steps to heal.

Find the root

To start, draw a card to help you identify and reflect on an issue that is deep-rooted in your family life. This issue may have cast a shadow over your childhood, your growth, and even your adult approach to what family can be. The Five of Pentacles might urge you to reflect on how your family's socio-economic situation affected your life, while the Lovers card could be about the ways in which the marriage and partnerships that define your family have affected you.

Explore the consequences

Next, draw cards in two horizontal parallel lines. The top three cards represent the consequences of the generational issue for your family. Some of these will undoubtedly be negative – the Three of Swords here could acknowledge pain and betrayal that occurred because of the themes that came up in the first card. But keep an open mind for how some consequences may have resulted in strengths – the Four of Wands may be a reminder of the value your family places on celebrating any small win.

The next three cards offer a chance to dive deep into your own personal experience with generational shadows, flaws, and traumas. Here you're looking at what your family's experience has done to, and for, you.

Move forward

The last card will help you decide what to do with your understanding of these generational issues. The Fool drawn here could suggest striking out on your own journey, free of family expectations. Justice or Judgment could encourage you to address issues with your family in order to move forward.

1. A generational shadow or trauma that I've inherited

2, 4, & 6. The consequences of this shadow/trauma on my family

3, 5, & 7. The consequences of this shadow/trauma on me

8. One small thing I can do to heal myself/my family

CONFLICT

In the spirit of being honest with ourselves and shining a light on our shadows this season, here's a spread to help you acknowledge your own role in a conflict – no matter how big, how small, or how complicated – so that you can focus more on moving forward than on covering up your weak spots.

Take a moment

Before you draw any cards, take a moment to meditate on whatever conflict you're currently in the midst of – it could be a simple disagreement with a partner over household duties, a serious moral debate with a friend, colleague, or family member, or anything in between. It could even be a conflict within yourself.

This spread is particularly ripe for deep journaling, so I recommend having a notebook on hand and writing your way through the spread at length.

Explore the conflict

Once you've made some initial notes and are clear on the conflict you want to explore through this spread, you can choose to either draw the first card of this spread at random to represent the conflict, or select a card from your deck that best mirrors the conflict in your eyes.

Ask yourself these questions in response to that first card:

- What can this card teach me about the conflict I'm facing?

- How does this card shine a light on something I may be avoiding when it comes to the conflict I'm dealing with?

- In what way can the energy of this card, which represents my current conflict, actually offer advice on how to move beyond the issue at hand?

Take action

Move through the rest of the card positions, shuffling your deck each time before drawing a new card. Write down at least a couple of sentences in response to each card as you go.

The final card will help you to decide on one thing that is within your control when it comes to solving the conflict. Using this card for guidance, write down one action you will take, inspired by this card, and set a deadline for when you will take that action.

1. The conflict
2. How my actions perpetuate the conflict
3. The person/thing I'm in conflict with
4. How that person/thing perpetuates the conflict
5. One thing within my control to help solve this conflict

SHADOW

CHOICE

Understanding the war within yourself can help you to make more informed and meaningful choices. This is a great spread to use when you feel frozen in a big decision, especially one that feels bound up in your personal values or identity.

Lay out your options

To prepare for this spread, think about the choice you hope this spread will help you make, and the two main directions in which the choice could lead you (e.g., quit my job or keep my job). You might want to write these options down, and have a think, before you draw any cards, about how each option captures both your 'shadow' side and your 'light' side. If using shadow and light in this context is confusing, think of your shadow side as the part of you that you keep hidden, and your light side as your 'ideal' version of yourself. Then, shuffle your deck and draw the first two cards. What can they teach you about what lies behind the choice you're facing?

Listen to light and shadow

Let's say I'm using this spread to decide if I should split with a partner. If I draw the Page of Wands for the first card, it could mean I feel restless about my relationship because I want a deeper, more passionate connection that I'm not currently getting. So, my 'light' side doesn't necessarily want to leave my partner, but it does want something more meaningful.

If I then draw the Five of Pentacles to represent what my 'shadow' side wants to choose, it could mean that my shadow side is currently after a little bit of self-destruction. Something within me wants to deprive myself. Knowing these things, I'm more armed to make an informed, thoughtful decision about my relationship.

Be upfront with yourself

The rest of the prompts in this spread will help you to dive deeply into what the two choices in front of you really look like – both for better and for worse. By being upfront with yourself and examining the potential consequences of both your options, you can distance yourself from the idea that there is a 'right' and 'wrong' choice, a 'dark' or 'light' choice. With more clarity and less judgment, you'll be able to move towards a choice you are confident in.

1. What your light side wants to choose
2. What your shadow side wants to choose
3. The best outcome of what your light side wants
4. The worst outcome of what your light side wants
5. The best outcome of what your shadow side wants
6. The worst outcome of what your shadow side wants
7. Advice for moving forward

SHADOW

CONFIDENCE

In this sweet and simple spread, the prompts will guide you through a series of questions to help you step out from beneath shadows of doubt or fear and into the light of your own, well-deserved confidence.

Observe the patterns

For the first prompt, shuffle and then draw the card at the very bottom of the deck. For the second card, draw from the top. Shuffle again and do the same, drawing from the bottom of the deck for the third prompt, and the top for the fourth card.

After you've laid the full spread out, take a minute to make note of the whole picture - are there any patterns or interesting connections that stand out to you?

Reveal what you're hiding

Once you're acquainted with the overall makeup of the spread, focus in on the first card, which represents something you're hiding from.

The Four of Wands here could mean that you're avoiding celebrating your wins - maybe because you don't think they're worthy enough, or you're superstitious about feeling too proud of yourself. Meanwhile the Ten of Swords tells the opposite story - you're hiding from the possibility of defeat or pain.

Whatever card you draw, take in the top-line message and move on to the second card, which will help you better understand what to do with this knowledge.

Next up, focus on the second card to help you understand how that recognition can help you to feel more confident facing the thing you've been hiding from.

Acknowledge and reframe

The fourth and final card can help you develop an action plan. Now that you have a better awareness of what you're hiding and have done the work of acknowledging and reframing it, you can move forward.

1. Something you're hiding from
2. How to acknowledge what you're hiding from
3. How this acknowledgment can help you gain confidence
4. How that confidence will help you step into the light and stop hiding

Cycle of Shadow

---✦---

In her poem, *A Certain Slant of Light*, Emily Dickinson – a writer I think was intimately in tune with her own shadow – describes a specific quality of light on winter afternoons as oppressive, a 'Seal of Despair / an imperial affliction' that gives her a 'Heavenly Hurt'. The poem, which I first read two decades ago in my teens, whispered to me as I reflected on this Season of Shadow, about the nuanced nature of light and shade. The way that in some contexts – in a certain slant – light can be just as painful, just as oppressive as shadow.

In the final stanza, Emily drives home the complex relationship between light and shadow, describing the way that even 'Shadows - hold their breath' when the oppressive winter light is cast on them.

Shadows, she suggests, hide from light as much as we hide from shadows. And both shadow and light, in their way, capture the best and worst of us. In both, there is nothing - and somehow everything - to fear. If shadow and light are two sides of the same coin, so too are the repression and exposure each propagates. It all hurts, so we might as well embrace it all - the light parts and the shadow.

Journal prompts

Take some time to meditate on your own relationship to light and shadow, through the lens of the poem and beyond.

Ask yourself:

- What does it mean to embrace my light and dark parts?
- How have my light and dark parts brought me both joy and pain?
- How have I come to better understand both my light and my dark parts this season?

A TAROT MANTRA FOR SHADOW WORK

Finish this Season of Shadow by distilling the most powerful takeaways into a mantra that you can carry with you into the next. Look to the tarot cards which have affected you most deeply over the season - or to the card you first drew to represent your shadow - to inform what you write.

If you're not sure what your mantra could be, here are a few you could work with:

A shadow mantra inspired by the Devil

I see and accept myself, warts, vices, problems, and all. I challenge myself to change for the better, but I offer myself grace and love no matter what.

A shadow mantra inspired by Judgment

What is buried within me is not rotten, it deserves my attention, my warmth, my light.

A shadow mantra inspired by the Moon

Just like the Moon, which experiences periods of full brightness, new darkness, and everything in between, I accept both light and shadow as crucial elements of my life journey.

A shadow mantra inspired by the High Priestess

I am brave enough to see the dark parts of myself, to sit with them, to honour them, to take the wisdom I need from them.

Write your chosen mantra on a sticky note and put it above a light switch in your house, to remind yourself of the dual nature of light and shadow.

Refer back whenever you find yourself judging parts of yourself, or even when you feel particularly affected by the shadow sides of others.

REFLECTIONS

As your Season of Shadow comes to a close, use this spread to look back over the experience of the past few months spent marinating in your own shadow. How has it felt, to peer underneath the surface of yourself? Do you have the answers you need, or do you have more questions?

Review your Shadow season

Take time to reflect on the prompts for this spread; consider journaling through them before you even draw cards. Then, when you're ready, shuffle your deck and lay out the three cards, one to represent what you've learned this season, one to represent the ways in which you embraced your shadows, and one to represent how you challenged your shadows this season.

Gain fresh insight

Check in on how each card adds depth and fresh insight to what you've journaled about. How does each card challenge what you thought, and how does each card validate your experience?

Think about how the answers to each question posed by this spread offer opportunity for you to celebrate yourself and all that you've learned. For each thing you've learned, embraced and challenged, invent a little reward you can give yourself to celebrate that progress.

Integrate light and shadow

Consider pulling a final card – one that captures you, in all of your shadow and light. Let this card guide you into the next season with awareness, balance, and the knowledge that your lightest and your most shadowy parts are two halves of a much bigger, more nuanced whole than words can ever truly describe.

1. What did I learn about my shadow self this season?
2. How did I embrace my shadow?
3. How did I challenge my shadow?

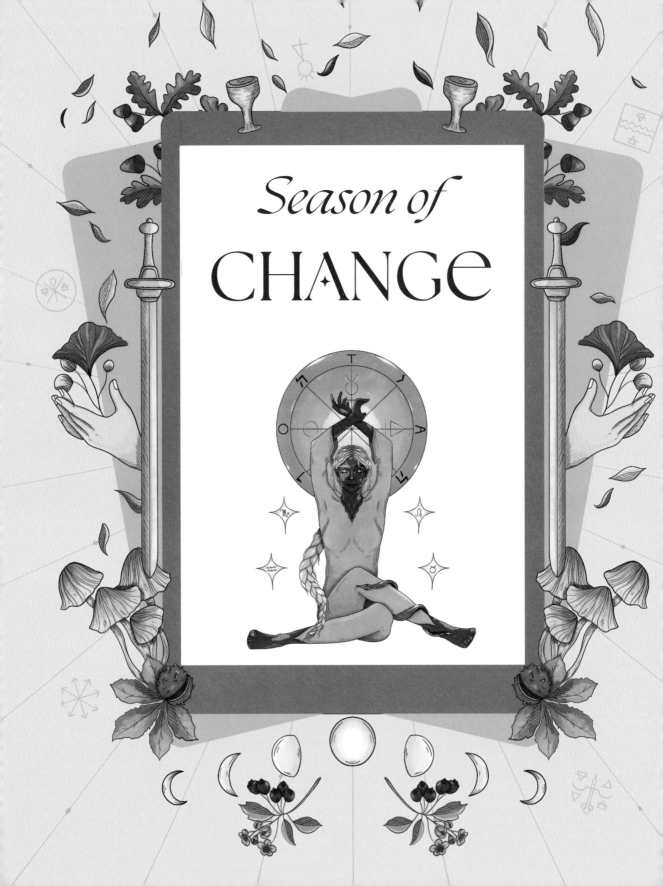

The famous missionary Mother Teresa once summed up her philosophy like this: 'I alone cannot change the world, but I can cast a stone across the waters to create many ripples.'

Change rarely matches this description when it's happening to us in the moment. When an unbidden change disrupts our lives, it feels cataclysmic – it's nothing like the calm image of ripples blooming outwards on the water's surface. At the opposite end of the spectrum, when we want to make change, it can be hard to even see the small ripples we've created through our actions.

But change is happening all around us, all the time. Good changes, bad changes, and neutral ones we forget to take note of. The sun rises and sets, meals start and end, moments of activity fade into moments of rest. Already, in working through this book, you've been through two changes of season. Cast your memory back over the experience, and consider what ripples have started to appear since you began your Season of Growth.

As you move through this Season of Change, I hope you'll build up a tool kit for looking at the ripple effects of change in your life. For stepping back and seeing your ocean of experience for the vast, resilient, adaptable, living thing that it is. I also hope you'll feel empowered by just how effective even the smallest acts toward change can be, once you take into account the idea that one little movement can set off ripples. Because this season isn't just about weathering change, it's about creating it.

With that in mind, before you move on to the spreads, spend some time journaling or meditating on these questions to help you prepare for the Season of Change:

- What changes have I been through recently, and how have they affected me?
- What do I love about change, and what do I hate about it?
- What changes would I like to see as a result of this season – within me and within my community and environment?
- If I could make the first move towards one specific change in the next three months, what would it be?

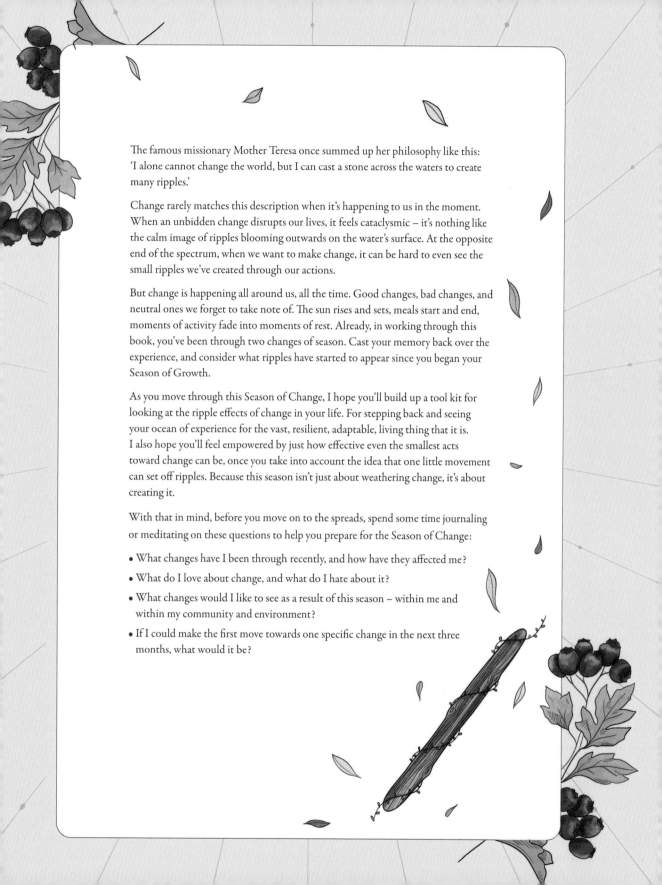

Change in the Tarot

The tarot is a masterclass in understanding and creating change. The Major Arcana, and every suit cycle, charts change – from little rises and falls to life-changing enlightenment. We see change happen fast – consider the tonal shift from Temperance to the Devil – and we see change happen slowly – the Fool's journey from innocence to wisdom happens over the course of 21 cards.

And change is often the whole point of reading tarot for ourselves. When we ask the cards for advice, what else are we looking for but permission and instruction to make change in our lives?

But even though we come to the tarot seeking change, the cards that signal change most prominently are two of the most feared cards in the deck: the Tower and Death. Both of these cards signal monumental change - within us and around us. Their imagery doesn't shy away from the fact that change can feel like a disaster, can feel like loss, can be terrifying.

But buried within this symbolism is the truth that change can also be exciting, invigorating, and life-giving. Whilst the Grim Reaper dominates the Death card in most traditional tarot decks, when you look closer, you might notice floral motifs, water, a sun, or harvest imagery in the illustration. Each of these elements represents the cyclical nature of change, and of death. What goes up, comes down and goes back up again. What grows, shrivels and fertilizes the ground for the next season. The card is ultimately an ode to, and acceptance of, change as a fact of life.

The Tower, which we discussed last season (see Shadow in the Tarot), also signifies the electricity of a sudden change. The experience of watching everything fall apart – and the opportunity this offers to rebuild. It's also a card that often represents epiphany. The lightning that strikes the Tower is a realization, a new way of seeing life. A change within you that tumbles everything that came before.

Reminder

This Season of Change is a natural evolution based on what you've gained through this book so far: Change is the sharp edge of Growth, but now that you're armed with a deeper knowledge of yourself following your Season of Shadow, you're ready to confront not just the exciting growth prospects of change, but the hard parts too.

Remember, as you move through this season and confront the changes you're forced to endure and adapt to, as well as the changes you want to create in yourself and the world, that you can take it one small step at a time. The ripple effect will take over from there.

INTENTIONS

It may be tempting to come into this season feeling like you're at the mercy of the changes happening to you, so this spread is designed to aid you in reclaiming your role as a change-maker rather than a change-responder.

Go beyond the Tower

To get started, shuffle your deck and then flip through until you find the Tower. Draw the card behind it and lay it out to answer the first prompt: A change I want to make within myself this season. Do this twice more, shuffling and locating the Tower, then drawing out the card behind it, until you've laid out all three cards in the spread.

Change what's in your power

Like many of the spreads throughout this book, I highly recommend journaling your way through this spread. Write in depth about how each card represents a meaningful answer to the spread prompts. Drawing Temperance for the first prompt, for example, may nudge you to explore why now is an important moment to make a change in terms of reducing your input or output – of money, of energy, of time... while in the second position, Temperance could suggest a similar reduction, but in physical resources like plastic, electricity, or fast fashion.

In either case, the card is a call to focus on making the most of what you have now. Write about how that suggestion makes you feel, what that change looks like in your life realistically, and what challenges you might come up against while you try to enact that shift.

Keep yourself afloat

While the first two spread prompts help you to identify the kinds of change you want to pursue this season, the final prompt is just as important, because it will help you reflect on what you need in order to keep yourself afloat while you make the change.

1. A change I want to make within myself this season
2. A change I want to make for my community this season
3. How I can be resilient in the face of change this season

RESOURCES

Changing our relationship to our resources can be hard, especially because that relationship is often one that we inherited. But change is possible, and can be not only refreshing but revolutionary. In this spread, you'll explore what changes you need to make when it comes to your resources, and how the change can benefit you.

Work with change

You may be doing this spread as a result of a change that's already happened in your resources – a professional change leading to more or less money, a new relationship meaning there's less time for you to spend on yourself or with friends, an illness or life event that's left you starved of energy, an unexpected inheritance giving you a new chance at financial freedom that you don't even know what to do with.

But maybe you just have a niggling feeling that something needs to change. Perhaps you don't like your spending habits, or you know you're giving too much time to things or people that don't mean enough to you. Or you could think of this spread as an insight to your relationship with your body as a resource.

Whatever resource you choose to focus on in this spread, the prompts will guide you toward the quality of change you need to make, and give you some context and support while you do that hard work of making change in your life.

Pay attention to themes

Shuffle your deck while thinking about the specific resource you want to focus on, then draw all four cards at once. Jot down some notes about your first impression of the overall spread – what stands out to you? Are there any obvious themes? If there are several Pentacles in the spread, this is likely a moment to reflect on how this resource affects you financially, professionally, or physically. Lots of Swords, on the other hand, might draw you to reflect on how the resource you're focusing on – and the way you use it – affects you mentally.

Discover a route to change

Then take time to reflect on each card, one at a time, and give yourself the space to explore what the spread can help you discover and action when it comes to changing your relationship with your resources.

1. How my relationship to my resources needs to change
2. Why this relationship needs to change
3. Something I'll gain from this change
4. How to be kind to myself while I make this change

SPIRIT

This spread is made for times when 'Tower moments' strike and force
you to confront change on a spiritual level... because sometimes
the beginning of enlightenment feels a lot like falling apart.

Confront big shifts

Whether you're confronting big shifts
in your personal beliefs, spiritual
approaches, or personal growth,
this spread can help you identify
the nature of the changes you're
facing on a spiritual level and frame
them in a way that feels helpful and
accessible rather than overwhelming.

Release old patterns

But just because a change in your
spiritual life can feel huge, that
doesn't mean it has to be. This
spread can be just as effective for
small changes. Maybe your spiritual
practice is making you realize there's
an old behavioural pattern you need
to let go of, or a relationship that no
longer serves you. Maybe it's calling
you to change the way you interact
with people at work, or to seek out a
new mentorship or community that's
in line with your path.

Centre yourself

This spread is designed to help
you tap in to the depths of your
spiritual side, so it's a good idea to
centre yourself first. Take a few quiet
moments and connect to yourself
on a spiritual level – depending on
your personal preference, this might

look like listening to some calming
music, meditating, or doing 'stream-
of-consciousness' journaling. Once
you've given yourself that space
to connect, shuffle your deck and
draw cards one by one, reflecting for
several moments on the potential
messages of each card as you go.

Seek out messages

As you draw each card, ask yourself:

- What element of this card do I feel
  most connected to on a soul level?
- How can that element inform the
  way this card makes me think about
  the spiritual change I'm facing?
- What other intuitive messages
  do I feel coming through
  while I look at these cards?

Find new wisdom

After you've finished with this spread,
take a picture or make a note, and
put a date in your diary to revisit
these cards in a month's time. When
you do, think about the ways the
spiritual change has played out, how
you were challenged, and what you
gained. What new wisdom can the
cards offer in retrospect?

1. A change that's taking place in my spiritual life
2. How this change will challenge me
3. How this change will benefit me

MIND

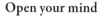

When you reconsider the way you think about the world, often as a result of a specific change you've witnessed or endured, it can be unsettling and embarrassing – discombobulating at the least. But you don't have to navigate the strange new land of your shifting mindset alone – you can let this spread guide you through.

Open your mind

To make the most of this spread, it does help to come with a semi-open mind. Look at this as a thought experiment to start - you're not signing a contract and agreeing to change your mind about anything just yet. You're simply exploring the possibility of what it might look like if you entertained another way of seeing your problems, your relationships, your life, or the world.

It may help, before you shuffle your deck and draw cards, to hold your deck to your heart and say these words: 'I'm open to the idea of change.'

Sit with that promise for a second, then shuffle, and lay out the first card in the spread to discover where you are in need of a change in mindset.

Note discomfort

Before you move on to laying out the next five cards, take some time to think really deeply about the first one. Think about how it connects to your life and experiences - explore the different things this card could be referring to.

While you're exploring what the card symbolizes for you, pay attention to any discomfort that arises. It's likely that the idea that brings up the most resistance is the area of life where you most need a shift in mindset.

Once you've got a handle on that first card and what it's asking of you, you can draw the next five cards a little more quickly if you like, jotting down their advice as you go.

Test a new mindset

Try accepting this mindset shift for a week - again thinking of it as a thought experiment. Get curious about what happens if you let someone else's opinion on a specific topic that came up in the reading win out. What are the boundaries around this mindset shift for you? Could it be something bigger that you might want to explore through future readings, conversations with trusted friends, or in therapy?

1. Where I need a change in mindset
2. Why this mindset shift is crucial right now
3. An action that will help me make this change
4. How this change in mindset will change my life as I know it
5. Where to look for support whilst I'm making this change
6. How to reward myself for embracing this change

CAREER

Inspired by the first half of the popular Celtic cross tarot spread, this spread is designed to help you identify and action meaningful changes in your professional life. It's helpful for big and small change alike – from asking for more responsibility in your current job to walking away from it entirely and retraining in a new field.

Make it happen

Only you will know what change you want, but the cards you draw can help you put language and structure to that change so that you can really set about making it happen.

Visualize what's in your way

Shuffle your deck and lay all the cards out at once, placing the second card horizontally directly on top of the first card, so you've creating a visual representation of what you want and what's in your way.

Reveal what you really want

Pay attention to the ways in which the cards you draw validate and challenge what you already know. The third card in the spread, which can help you identify what you really want from a change in your work life, can be particularly illuminating. You might think you want a pay rise, but drawing the Eight of Cups or the Seven of Wands here could be a sign that what you really want is to get out of there entirely. Whatever card you draw here will shine a light on feelings about your career that are normally stuck in the subconscious.

Review past experiences

The fourth card, which is designed to help you reflect on past career experiences that have led you to this moment, can also be really useful for context. It may remind you that your current work situation echoes a previous experience with bad management, or that in your last job you developed a skillset that's now being exploited or under-utilized.

Make an action list

After you've reflected on the cards and what they can tell you about the changes you want to make in your career, try converting the reading into key actions. The fifth card, which offers advice on your next steps, is a good place to start, but think also about what you can do to turn the learnings from the other cards into solid steps, too.

You can draw this spread anytime you feel called, but it's very much one worth returning to when you're preparing for a quarterly or annual review, or need to plan your own change in response to other shifts taking place in your work life.

1. A change I want to make in my career
2. What's stopping me from making the change
3. What I really want from this change
4. How my past career experiences have brought me here
5. The next step I need to make toward this change
6. The energy this change will bring into my life

PLAY

In many ways, having a sense of play goes hand in hand with being adaptable to change. When we will play into our lives, we welcome experimentation, delight in the unexpected, and crave surprise. Too often, though, when we're faced with the pressures brought on by unwelcome change, play is the first thing we cut from our lives as we attempt to adapt.

Harness playfulness

Using this spread, you can harness playfulness as a helpful agent and balm for change. The prompts are designed to get you thinking about play as a tool for weathering and creating change, as well as caring for yourself through change.

Prepare with playtime

As usual for the play spreads, I recommend breaking out your brightest, merriest tarot deck for this one, and preparing to doodle and journal your way through the prompts with a light, open mind. It might help to prepare yourself with some playtime before you draw cards. You could try some of the following activities to get yourself in the zone:

- Create a collage about what play means to you.

- Hold a personal dance party to your favourite song.

- Write the silliest poem you can about a change you're currently facing, or one you want to make.

- Do something that gets you messy – finger paint, sculpt, garden.

When you're feeling sufficiently connected to your most playful side, shuffle your deck and lay out the cards one at a time.

Make a game of it

Continuing on in a playful vibe, try responding to the cards using quick-fire word association: what does the card make you think about, and what does that thing make you think about, and so on? Do this for each card, and then reflect back on what you've written down, exploring how it relates back to the change you're currently facing.

Consider keeping the playful vibes alive even longer by making some art about the insight you've gained and what you've discovered by working through this spread.

1. How play can help me adapt to change
2. What I can learn about change through playfulness
3. One way I can change up my current approach to play

CHANGE

FRIENDSHIP

Whenever we face change in our lives, our relationships have to play catchup. This can often lead to tension; it can also lead to more change.

Welcome new eras of your friendships

Friendships are constantly affected by the shifting tides of life for all parties involved. A move may mean that the way you keep in touch shifts from real life meetups to online ones. A lifestyle change may mean that you move away from nights out and invite your friends for morning coffee dates instead.

Marriages, divorces, career moves, sobriety, children, illness – all of these big life events that may happen to you and your friends demand that your relationships adapt. And while we all hope that adaptation through change brings us closer to our friends, that our relationships change for the better, it's important to be prepared for our friendships to ebb and flow with the changes we face in life.

Zoom out on change

Use this spread to zoom out on the way change is affecting your friendships now, and consider how you can lean into those changes for the good of the relationship. You'll also gain insight into how you can be a friend to yourself through this time, no matter what happens.

Think differently

Shuffle your deck and go ahead and lay out all the cards at once. Take stock of the images in front of you, and make a note if any of the cards particularly remind you of a friend, or of the situation you currently find yourself in. Then work through the prompts and the corresponding cards to help you step back and think about your friendships differently in this moment of change.

Explore opposing perspectives

The cards in positions two and three can tell you a lot about whether or not you and your friend are aligned in the face of change. If, for example, you're looking for insight into a friendship that's been cooling because one of you is in a new relationship, and you draw the Lovers card for yourself but the Eight of Swords for your friend, you can be sure that you're bringing very different energies into the relationship right now.

Let the cards give you the tools to grant space and grace to your friendships, and focus on the final card, which will help you be kind to yourself, no matter how a change affects your friendships.

1. A change I'm facing in my friendships
2. How this change is affecting me
3. How the change is affecting my friend(s)
4. How the change can make my friendships stronger
5. How to care for myself during this change

ROMANCE

Whether you're stepping into a new relationship, leaving an old one behind, changing the terms of engagement with your current partner in some way, or something else, this spread is here to help you get a fresh perspective on the changes happening in your love life now.

Open your heart

It helps to come to this spread with an open heart and mind. You may want to prepare yourself with some stream-of-consciousness journaling around your hopes, dreams, and concerns for your love life. It's also a good idea to give yourself some love before drawing this spread, whether that's treating yourself to your favourite indulgence, lighting a candle and having a soak, heading off to a restorative yoga class, or checking in with the support systems beyond your romantic life, like a trusted friend or family member.

When you're feeling expansive and in a loving state of mind, shuffle your deck and then lay the cards out one by one, so you can give each card your full attention when you place it on the table.

Look for a meaningful shift

For the first prompt, you'll draw a card to reflect the current change you're facing in your love life. If you're going through a breakup or entering a new relationship, you'll know very well what that change is, so think of this card as an indicator of how this external change is going to create a meaningful shift within you and/or your relationship. For instance, if you've just got engaged and you draw the Three of Pentacles, you know that the external change is your engagement, but the Three of Pentacles is a reminder that not only are you and your partner in love, but you are now building something together, and now is a moment to think about how planning a wedding and a future as a married couple changes the dynamic between you.

See opportunity

If you're experiencing a breakup and draw the Judgement card for the first position, you know that this change is the end of the relationship. But Judgement invites you to go deeper – to see this as an opportunity to resurrect a version of yourself that perhaps was buried beneath the pressure to prioritize being a partner first, and yourself second.

The rest of this spread helps to unpack the message of the first card, allowing you to process the change and make a plan for the next step of your romantic life.

1. A change I'm facing in my romantic life
2. How that change is affecting me emotionally
3. How I can take care of myself in the face of this change
4. A new energy this change is bringing into my life
5. How I can embrace this new energy

FAMILY

In the friendship and romance spreads for change, we focused on navigating changes that are thrust upon us in those relationships. In this family spread, we're going to take a more proactive approach and allow the cards to guide us toward the changes we'd like to make within our families.

Brainstorm for change

Draw the first card and jot down a few notes on what the card can tell you about your family life right now. What rings true? What surprises you?

Before drawing again, fill up a piece of paper by brainstorming everything you'd like to change – for better or worse – about your family life at the minute. Use what you learned from the first card in the spread, and also draw on your recent experience with your family, and how you've felt.

Be flexible

Being elastic with your definition of change for this spread is a good idea. As you're brainstorming, remember that while change might be an obvious physical development, like moving to a new home or bringing a new member into the family, it could also be a behavioural change. Maybe you want to start spending more time with your children, being more proactive about shared chores in the house, or perhaps it's time to change the way or the frequency with which you interact with a family member.

Find a good match

Once you've done that quick brainstorm, you can either read it back, circle the specific change you'd most like to make and keep that in mind while you draw the rest of the cards for the spread, or you can go ahead and draw the second card and see which of the things you wrote down feels like the best match for the card.

Gain perspective

You can go on to draw the last two cards together at the same time, and use them to help you gain context and perspective around what making a change in your family life could mean for you and your family.

1. My family life now
2. A change I'd like to make in my family life
3. How that change will affect me
4. How that change will affect my family

  CHANGE

CONFLICT

In a lot of ways, change and conflict are two sides of the same coin – they come as a package deal. Unexpected or unwanted change usually causes some kind of conflict, and conflict always forces some kind of change.

Conflict and change

For this spread, you'll be looking closely at the relationship between the changes and the conflicts you're experiencing in your life right now.

Start by shuffling your deck, and divide it into four piles. Draw a card for the first prompt from the first pile, one for the second prompt from the second pile, and so on until you've laid out four cards. Because this spread is about the relationship between conflict and change, look first at the cards as a whole and gauge their relationship to each other. How do you think the cards you've drawn are working together to help you better understand and navigate the change and conflict you're currently dealing with?

Draw out themes

Now focus on each card individually, seeking what it can tell you about the prompt. Look out for themes of conflict and change in the illustration. For example, if you're using a fully illustrated deck and draw the Nine of Wands for the second position, then exploring the way that conflict is illustrated within this card can be really helpful for your interpretation.

In many traditional versions of the Nine of Wands, we see an injured figure clinging to one staff, while the other eight staffs loom behind him. We can see – through the injuries to the figure's body and the look on their face as they cast their eyes backward at the menacing eight wands - that they feel hunted.

When you bring that impression into your reading, you may be reminded that you've recently felt like everyone turned against you at work or in a social setting, and you can recognize how that experience is contributing to the conflict you're dealing with. Knowing and understanding how that experience of change is affecting you is one way you can better empower yourself to solve problems thoughtfully.

Reclaim autonomy

While the first two positions in this spread focus on helping you understand the root of the conflict, positions two and three are all about helping you move past the conflict in a healthy way. You can use what you learn from these cards to take back some autonomy, and plan to make positive changes.

1. A conflict I'm dealing with now
2. A change that put this conflict in motion
3. A change I can make to move beyond the conflict
4. A change I may need to accept as a result of this conflict

CHOICE

When change occurs, we have to choose how we respond to it, and that's exactly what this spread is designed to help you do. It's a good spread to turn to when you feel cornered into making a decision and need a moment to step back and consider your options.

Plan ahead and take your time

You can also use this spread as a planning tool – a change doesn't have to have happened yet for you to want to lay out what your life might look like when it does.

This is a big spread, with lots of cards, so you may want to work through it slowly – give yourself at least an hour to make sure that you're giving each card the time it deserves.

With busy spreads like this, I like to make time to revisit them on several occasions over the course of a week. I might draw all the cards on a Sunday evening, but I won't consider the reading finished until I've come back to the cards for 20 minutes or so on Monday, Tuesday, and Wednesday.

Identify the change

The first card in this spread will help you identify the change that's precipitating the choice you're preparing to make. You can use the suit of the card to help you narrow down what area of your life the change might be affecting: drawing a Pentacle means the change is probably related to work or finance; drawing a Cup means the change is probably related to your emotional life or your relationship; a Wand indicates you're dealing with some kind of change or epiphany about your spiritual or creative life; and a Sword probably means that a serious hardship has come your way.

A new chapter

If you draw a Major Arcana in the first position, the cards are probably telling you that you're entering a whole new chapter of your life, and that the theme of the card is the lesson you'll need to learn.

The following six cards will lay out your options for responding to the change. Feel free to get creative here, and use them as a brainstorm, as jumping off points to lead you toward solutions that feel right, or consider ways you can combine them to get the best outcome.

You'll close the spread by drawing two final cards to help you consider how to use these options to make an informed choice that sits well with your needs, and matches your gut feelings about what to do next.

1. A change that's forcing me to make a choice
2. Option one
3. Option two
4. Option three
5. Option four
6. Option five
7. Option six
8. What to prioritize when making this choice
9. What my intuition is telling me about the choice

CONFIDENCE

One way to define confidence is that it's the knowledge you can use to adapt to whatever comes your way. In that respect, change is a key ingredient in the building of confidence.

Change to grow

This spread can help you harness your response to change for the sake of growing confidence. Consider it a field guide for healthy adaptation.

You can use this spread to help you reflect on any kind of change you're undergoing, whether it's a change that's been thrust upon you, one you've put into motion yourself, or (most commonly, let's be honest) a mix of the two. You can also use it as a follow up to any of the previous spreads from this season.

Explore what you'll gain

The best way to use this spread is to lay it out in two parts. Start by drawing the first two cards, and spend some time exploring what they're telling you.

Say you're focusing this spread on how a current job change can build your confidence. If you draw the Page of Pentacles for the first card and the Seven of Swords for the second card, you could use these as prompts to explore how this job change can help you gain new skills and knowledge that you've missed out on by trying to 'get away' with doing the least in past jobs.

Validate yourself

After you've become familiar with the message you feel is speaking to you most strongly in the first two cards, it's time to draw cards three and four. These cards are all about giving you the affirmation and validation you need to weather the change you're facing. For example, if you draw the Devil and the Six of Cups here, you could interpret their advice like this: the Devil offers pretty solid advice for embracing the change – you've got to untangle yourself from past ways of working that are no longer going to cut it.

The Six of Cups makes up for the Devil's tough love with a reminder that you're actually very good at sharing your own knowledge and skillset. With this in mind, the solution could be to set up a skillshare program at your new work. Or maybe it's about giving yourself permission to be the student rather than the teacher in this new role – a meaningful but difficult identity shift.

1. How the change I'm facing can help me grow confidence
2. What's keeping me from seeing this change as an opportunity
3. One way I can better embrace this change
4. One strength I already have to help me weather this change

Cycle of Change

In his novel, *The Graveyard Book*, Neil Gaiman wrote: 'You're always you, and that don't change, and you're always changing, and there's nothing you can do about it.' This statement, which feels both beautiful and fatalistic, is missing an important element, if you ask me... Yes. You're always changing. And no, there's nothing you can do about that. But there is so much you can do *with* that.

I hope that as a result of the journey you've undertaken this season, changes both big and small have come about. I hope that you've been able to practice responding to change, and making it; that you've welcomed change as part of your lifecycle, and recognized it as an opportunity to grow into yourself and the world around you.

We live in a time rife with change – both for better and worse, nothing stays the same for long. Our culture, our environment, our lives change at breakneck speed. But when we let ourselves off the hamster wheel for a second, even if only in our own minds, we can start to think about what we can do with those changes, instead of what they do to us. The tarot spreads you've practiced throughout this season can be meaningful companions in that work – helping you to pause, reflect, and consider how you want to work with the change that's occurring, and how you might make the change you want to see.

Journal prompts

Take some time now to reflect on how your relationship to change has, well... changed over the course of the last few months. Explore the ways in which you've worked with change and for change, and what that means for you next.

Ask yourself:

- What does change mean to me today?
- How has my response to change evolved this season?
- If change happens and there's nothing I can do about that, what can I decide to do with it instead?
- In what ways can I embrace my ever-changing self?

TAROT MANTRAS FOR CHANGE

To help you embrace change in all its forms, consider creating a mantra that captures the most meaningful lessons you learned this season. Use the tarot cards that have affected you most deeply over the season – or look back to Death and the Tower – to inform what you write.

If you're not sure what your mantra could be, feel free to use one of mine:

A change mantra inspired by Death

Changes, both good and bad, are essential parts of life. I acknowledge the hard and the beautiful parts that come with moving through change, and I give myself permission to mourn what was as I move into a new chapter.

A change mantra inspired by the Eight of Pentacles

I am willing to do the small daily work towards the big changes I want to see. I trust that every little bit I do creates a ripple effect, and that the change I want to see in the world and in myself is possible through my effort.

A change mantra inspired by the Tower

When change strikes, I look for the opportunity it creates for me. I open myself up to the possibility, and the optimism, of constant rebuilding.

A change mantra inspired by the Aces of the Tarot

I embrace change as a signal of new beginnings, and I look for the blessings a new start can bestow.

Use your phone to set up a reminder so that your chosen change mantra pops up at moments of change in your calendar: New Year's, a birthday, the seasonal shifts, or around a big life change you have planned. You can also refer back to this mantra whenever you find yourself faced with change.

REFLECTIONS

As your Season of Change draws to a close, look to this last spread as an opportunity to reflect back on your experiences these past few months and note the changes that have taken place.

Go back to the start

Before you draw cards for this spread, it's a good time to review the intention spread at the start of this season. If you made notes or took a photo of the cards you drew for that first spread, review them now and check in on how you feel you met those intentions over the past few months. Notice too, how those intentions may have changed and evolved as a result of working through the other spreads during this Season of Change.

Once you've refreshed your memory on your intentions, cast your eyes back over the prompts for this reflection spread and journal through them based on your experience. Then, draw a card for each prompt and consider how it ties your intentions and reflections from this season together.

Enrich your relationship to the cards

As a final exercise, flip through your deck until you find the Tower and Death cards. Draw these out and spend some time exploring these cards now, as you bring this season to a close. Think about the way

that the cards you've pulled for this reflection spread can enrich your relationship with the Tower and Death moving forward.

Ask yourself:

- What still scares me about these cards?

- How can the lesson I've learned about change this season help me embrace Tower and/or Death energy in my life?

- What were my biggest Tower and/or Death moments this season?

- How do the cards I've drawn for this reflection spread offer different ways of thinking about the Tower and Death?

Wrap up by writing a short letter to the version of yourself you were at the beginning of this season. Tell yourself about all of the ways you've embraced change and grown from it this season. Share your biggest encouragements, learnings, and advice with your past self. Tuck this away and save it for a rainy day when you've forgotten just how resilient you are in the face of change.

1. What change did I make within myself this season?
2. What change did I make for my community this season?
3. What lesson did I learn about change this season?

Season of

CARE

The tarot is a tool for knowing yourself, and knowing yourself is the first step to caring for yourself. At least that's the idea that Plato posits in his *Socratic Dialogue, Alcibiades I*. 'Care for your psyche,' he writes, 'Know thyself, for once we know ourselves, we may learn how to care for ourselves.'

This season, we're following Plato's advice, and then some. We're tapping into the tarot in order to know ourselves, so that we can care not only for ourselves, but for the people in our lives, and for the world around us.

Exploring care is a big task, because the word is a wide umbrella: care is getting a good night's sleep, eating a balanced diet, spending quality time with the people we love, giving back to our community. Care is being a citizen of the earth. Care is giving time to our passions, investing in our future. Care is seeking mental health resources when – and even before – we find ourselves in need of them. Care is saying no to some things and yes to others. Care is relieving pressure, and rejecting stereotypes that don't feel good to us. Care can mean leaving, or staying. For each of us, in every moment, the care we need, and the care we have to offer, is completely unique to us.

For that reason, one of the best ways to kick this season off in a spirit of care is to define what care means to you right now. Like Plato said, you've got to know yourself to care for yourself – so let's dig deep into what you know about your personal relationship with care, as it stands right now.

Spend a few minutes journaling about your feelings towards care – all the good and the bad that come with the word, and then ask yourself these questions:

- What makes me feel cared for?
- How do I care for myself?
- How do I want to care for others?
- If I could improve one thing about my relationship with care this season, what would it be?

Care in the Tarot

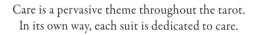

Care is a pervasive theme throughout the tarot.
In its own way, each suit is dedicated to care.

Pentacles prioritize care of the body, the Earth, and our resources. As we saw in the Season of Growth, cards like the Seven and Eight of Pentacles are particularly good illustrations of a caretaking energy. In the Seven, we see a farmer contemplating his crop. The Eight puts care in action, offering an example of what it looks like to do our work with care. Even a card like the Four of Pentacles captures an aspect of care – the figure may simply be trying to care for more than they have the realistic resources to cope with.

The Cups depict what it means to care for our own emotions, and to hold space for the care of others. The King and Queen of Cups are paragons of caring leadership, while the Six of Cups is a beautiful ode to community care. The Four and Five, meanwhile, encourage us to make space and offer care to ourselves and others in the midst of difficult times.

The Wands capture the care and feeding of our spirit. The early cards in this suit, like the Two, Three, and Four, are nods to dreaming big and celebrating our achievements – essential forms of care for our creative side. The later cards, especially the Nine and Ten, warn against what happens when we stretch ourselves too thin, and forget to prioritize what brings us joy.

And the harrowing journey through the Swords suit is a reminder that we need to balance our hard times out with care. The Four of Swords is a call for rest and retreat, while the Three, Six, and Ten all acknowledge in their own ways that self-care is hardly a picnic. Doing what we need to do for ourselves can be a gnarly business, and no suit embraces that truth more than the Swords.

The Major Arcana as a whole is a journey towards deep, soul care – but a few particular cards stand out when we talk about care. The Star is the quintessential care card within the tarot. It's a literal illustration of what it means to fill your own well, and how, in doing so you will create new depths to draw on, and gain strength to bring back into the world.

If the Star is a card about giving care to ourselves, then the Empress is a card that captures the energy of giving care to others, and receiving care from them, too. The Empress is typically represented as an earth mother or divine feminine archetype. In one of my favourite tarot decks, Ari Wesiner's genderless Transient Light Tarot, the Empress is renamed and simply titled 'The Nurturer.' It's illustrated by a pearl cushioned in the protection of an oyster - a reminder that care offers the conditions for beauty.

For me, the most important Major card when it comes to care is Strength. This card, which traditionally depicts a feminine figure taming a beast, illustrates the duality implicit in the act of giving care - the essential combination of gentleness and pure grit. In French, the card is titled 'La Force,' and even more than strength, I think this captures the sheer willpower that care requires. To care for ourselves, and to care for others, is not for the faint of heart.

Reminder

This season is all about care, and while you're learning about your relationship with giving and receiving it, make a special effort to care for yourself as you move through the season.

You may find that by diving deep into gaining a better understanding of what care means for you, you have less time to give care to others. You may need more time to yourself for discovery and change, which naturally results in less time for others. When guilt creeps in, remind yourself that this season is an investment in your long-term relationship with care, and that your loved ones will benefit from you taking this time.

Audre Lorde said it best when she called self-care a form of self-preservation. While her words have been twisted in recent years to sell commercialized versions of self-care, you can take the liberty right now to reclaim them, and to think about self-care as an act that is ultimately in service of the care you offer others. You can't pour from an empty cup - look no further than the suit of Cups to tell you that much - so make sure yours is full to the brim, and never forget that you deserve that.

INTENTIONS

This spread is all about helping you start off your Season of Care on the right foot. It's designed to help you define what care will look and feel like for you this season, so that you can get down to the task of caring instead of just thinking about care.

Set goals with care

By drawing cards for this spread, you'll look at three crucial aspects of care you need to be clear on as you move into this season: the care you give yourself, the care you give others, and your overarching relationship to what it means to care and be cared for.

Return to care

Care looks and feels different for everyone. And it even looks different for us individually depending on the time of day, week, month, and year. That's why I recommend checking in with this spread regularly throughout your Season of Care.

You can return to the same intention cards frequently and journal about how your relationship with each card is growing and changing throughout the season. Or you can draw fresh cards for the spread daily or weekly – all you need to do is sub out the language. So you can ask the cards 'How can I care for myself today?' instead of 'How can I care for myself this season?'

Take action

Whether you use this spread once or 50 times, the most important thing is that you carry out the care that you've learned that you, and the people in your life, need. Any time you pull cards for this spread, take five minutes to draft a list of small actions you can take to prioritize care in the coming hours, days, or weeks.

1. How can I care for myself this season?

2. How can I care for others this season?

3. What is the biggest lesson I need to learn about care?

RESOURCES

Think of this spread as the 'Marie Kondo' method of tarot spreads. It's here to help you identify the things in your life that belong, and re-examine those things that may, in reality, be less of a resource and more of a burden.

Share with care

Here's an example: let's say that in the first card position I draw the Three of Cups. This card is probably here to tell me that my version of caring for my resources is to share them with my friends and community. It would be right – I love to share books, meals, time, and energy with my friends. Sharing increases the love I feel for the people in my life.

Drawing the Queen of Cups for the second card position would validate the first. That Queen of Cups confirms that I get energy from being generous, from giving and loving.

Challenge yourself

But this isn't a purely lovey-dovey spread. It also looks into the more ambivalent relationship you may have with your resources. In the third position, you're invited to reflect on a resource you don't really care about. When I practised this spread myself, the Ten of Swords came up. This suggests that there's something I feel I've worked very hard to build, but which may not actually be getting my genuine care and attention.

Release distractions

Finally, your fourth card is a gut punch – here's a resource you may be focused on, one which you may care an awful lot about, but one which doesn't really offer you the care you need and deserve back. I drew the Nine of Wands for myself here, which to me meant that the resource I'm overly concerned about – the one that I care about way more than it cares about me – is other people's opinions and views on me and my work. The card points out the harsh reality that I spend too much time and energy – too many of my own valuable resources – being paranoid about critical success and failure, when the truth is that having success and accolades doesn't ultimately provide me with the care I need.

Reset your course

Having got to know how your resources, your care, and wellbeing intersect, jot down a few ideas for correcting course to take better care of yourself and your resources, or how to release those resources which don't really serve you.

1. How I care for my resources
2. How my resources provide care for me
3. A resource I don't care about
4. A resource that doesn't care for me

SPIRIT

So much of caring for ourselves is acknowledging our sore spots, so that we can be kind and gentle with them. In this spread, you'll face spiritual wounds head on. What that means depends on you, on your history, and on your spiritual practice and belief system.

Focus and explore

For me personally, caring for myself spiritually is tied up in being creative – in allowing my mind and heart to find themselves committed to paper. When I'm sore inside, the only way to heal is to write it down. Tarot cards are a tool for me too, of course. They help me focus and explore my thoughts so that I can get them down on paper, whether through journaling or writing fiction and poetry.

Honour your wounds

Your spiritual practice will look different than mine. It may involve meditation, worship, walking, spell-craft, gardening, singing, sex. This spread isn't really about the method of care - but if you need ideas, the second card is there to prompt you. What this spread is really about though, is helping you to recognize and honour the wounds your spiritual practice can help to heal.

Draw double

I've invited you to draw two cards each for the final two prompts. That's because I think these questions are particularly nuanced and it's good to give yourself more to work with. When you're reading two cards together for these prompts, think about the story you're seeing take shape - the exchange of ideas that the two cards together suggest. When I draw two cards together, I like to sketch out a conversation between the two of them, like a Socratic dialogue, and see what I learn from it.

Start a conversation

Let's say I drew the Fool and the Hanged One for positions three and four. I might imagine the two cards having a conversation about a time when I felt a risk I took trapped me, but how ultimately, that risk gave me a valuable new perspective regardless of the outcome. Try this technique yourself when working through this spread, and see how it opens up the possibilities and stories you tell yourself about spiritual care.

3 **4** **2** **5** **6**

1

1. Where I need spiritual care
2. How I can give spiritual care to myself
3 & 4. How that care can help me heal from the past
5 & 6. How that care will help me move forward into the future

MIND

Caring for our mental health is one of the most important, but often underrated, things we can do for ourselves as human beings. Becoming more in tune with the ups and downs of your mental health, exploring your unique experiences, and coming to a better understanding of your patterns and needs, can lead to a much fuller life overall.

Care for your mind

When we care for our minds, we care for the signal centre of our entire body. Our mind is the decision-maker, the task driver, the boss-in-charge of our entire human experience. So, if it isn't cared for, I don't think it's really possible to function, let alone care for our bodies, our homes, our work, or anyone else in our lives.

Connect to your breath

Before you draw cards for this spread, take 30 seconds to a minute and close your eyes. Connect to your own breath, and mentally scan your body from head to toe. Give yourself a little shake, then shuffle your deck to draw cards.

Ask for help

The final prompt in this spread, 'Where or who I can ask for help to care for my mental health,' is so, so important. I designed this spread to help you take action to care for your mind, but I believe that the best action any of us can take for our mental health is to build support networks. This card position will help you think about where or who can give you that support – or the kind of qualities you need from that support, be it a therapist, friend, family member, or other counsellor.

Get a full spectrum of support

Tarot has been a huge help to me in caring for my mental health on a daily basis, but I also have a long-standing relationship with a therapist, and lots of friends dedicated to caring for their own mental health that set great examples for me. I want this full spectrum of support for you too, because you should never feel alone in the duty of care to your mind.

1. My mental state now
2. How I can care for myself in my current state
3. The consequences of not caring for my mind now
4. Where or who I can ask for help to care for mental health

CAREER

Caring for ourselves at work is hard, and part of the reason is because disconnecting from work these days – mentally and physically – can feel impossible. It's not uncommon anymore to feel unable to really disconnect and detangle yourself from work for days, weeks, months, even years at a time. The result of that endless grind is burn-out.

Confront burn-out

This spread is simple and direct, because when you're burnt out, an information overload is exactly what you don't need.

To start, shuffle your deck and draw the first card, which represents how you're experiencing burn-out right now. Give this card your full attention. Sit with it for up to five minutes. Get intimately acquainted with the imagery and what it brings up for you. Don't pressure yourself to find an answer, instead, let thoughts and observations about your experience arise gently. Feel free to just sit with these feelings, or to jot down your thoughts in a notebook if it helps you.

Find ways out

Once you've spent time with this first card, and gotten to know the various things it's saying to you, it's time to draw the second card, which will help you brainstorm ways of caring for yourself, and attitudes you can adopt to help you navigate burn-out.

Channel boss witch energy

If you draw the King of Pentacles for your first card, this could suggest that you're burnt out in your personal enterprises – a side hustle or a small business venture – or that a management position is overwhelming you. If you then draw the Queen of Wands, then the advice definitely isn't about commercial self-care. Instead, channel the card's Boss Witch energy: make a list of all the ways the Queen of Wands attitude can help you take the best care of yourself in the face of burn-out, for instance the Queen of Wands:

- *is not afraid to set boundaries or say no*
- *is not afraid to raise her prices or ask for that pay rise*
- *talks herself up, surrounds herself with the things that empower her*
- *knows the worth of her talent and her resources far beyond the job she's doing*
- *trusts that she'll land on her feet.*

Pin your list up somewhere you can see it while you're working, and refer to it when you need some extra TLC.

1. How I'm experiencing burn-out right now

2. How I can care for myself and recover

CARE

PLAY

Care is often lumped into two categories: work and rest. Caring for others, and sometimes ourselves, is hard work – cooking, cleaning, maintenance. And then for 'rest' there's the reduction of self-care to a commodity, which is more often than not something like candles, bubble baths, and steaming tea.

Care through play

It's easy to forget that one essential way we can care for ourselves is by approaching our lives with a sense of play. Take hobbies – a hobby gives you a break from the version of you at work, and in your relationships that's always striving to hit the next milestone – to get better, faster, stronger. A hobby is something you explore for love, for joy, for escape, for the pure sake of it. Whether it's some kind of creative or manual work, sport, or study, a hobby is the adult version of a toy box. You open it up, and give it your attention because you are craving play.

But you don't have to have an ongoing hobby to infuse your life with play either. Day trips to new places, concerts, literal play with the children or pets in your life – all of these are great ways to care for yourself through play, and when you do them with loved ones, you're offered the chance to care for your relationships through play, too.

Prioritize play

This spread is designed to help you prioritize play as a tool for care. The prompts will help you identify where and how play can provide you with essential care, and advice on how to bring that sense of play into your life.

Suit yourself

When you lay out this spread, pay attention to the suits you draw. Remember that each tarot suit corresponds to an element of the self: Pentacles is your work and family life, Swords is your mental life, Cups is your emotional life, and Wands is your creative and spiritual life. Let the suit you draw in the first position guide you towards where you need more playful care.

Let loose

If you draw a Major Arcana card first, focus on the ways the archetype of the card is preventing you from play. The Star may suggest you're too focused on 'rest and relax' self-care and you need to open up your care to include play, while the Magician could be telling you that your desire for power is keeping you from lightening up and letting loose.

1. Where I need more play in my life
2. How play helps me care for myself
3. One thing I can do to encourage play in my life

FRIENDSHIP

I consider my friends the first responders when I need care, and I think I play that role for many of them too. I hope you have close relationships that feel the same but even if you don't, this spread can be useful in identifying how you care for yourself while tending to the other people in your life.

Care for yourself like a friend

In fact, this spread is designed to remind you that as much it's important to show up for your 'Ride-or-Dies', it's always more important to show up for yourself first, so that the care you offer others doesn't drain the care you are responsible for giving yourself.

Set the tone

When laying out the spread, first shuffle and draw cards for card positions one and two. The first card prompt, 'Where I need care right now,' will set the tone for the spread, and give you a sense of what you need to focus on for yourself and what you're able to bring to the table for others. (If you're having a Tower or Hermit moment right now, you might want to limit the amount of energy you promise to other people, no matter what they may need.)

For that second card, you may have a specific friend in mind that you want to focus on in this reading. But if you don't, the card can help you narrow down which of your relationships – whether deep or casual – needs your attention the most. The Two of Cups might indicate that it's actually your partner or best friend that needs your attention, while the Three of Pentacles might hint that your work lunch buddy could use a little TLC.

Fill your own cup

The rest of the cards offer insight into how you can provide care – and you'll notice that while there's only one card offering advice on caring for your friend, there are a whole three cards about caring for yourself. That's because the old adage is true – you've got to love yourself first to be any good to anyone else.

Check in on yourself

Use this spread any time you feel like you're giving too much to others without looking after yourself, or as a more general check-in to help you be a good friend in a balanced way.

1. Where I need care right now
2. Where a friend needs care right now
3. How I can care for my friend
4, 5, & 6. How I need to care for myself

ROMANCE

It's good and right to look to your intimate relationships for the deepest wells of care. After all, we commit to other people because we know that the power of mutual care is a key component to survival.

Make care essential

But just because it's true that care is essential in a committed relationship, it doesn't mean that you always find the care you're looking for. Nor does it mean that you're able to provide the necessary depth of care for a partner, either.

Using this spread, you can reflect and course-correct when it comes to the role of care in your relationship. It's designed to give equal weight to three kinds of care - the care you need from your partner, the care they need from you, and the care you both have to give to your relationship, together.

Take stock of where you're at

Before you draw cards that explore those three types of care, the first two positions prompt you to draw cards to represent you and the partner you're exploring care with, respectively. Because before you can identify where you need to go together, you've got to take stock of where you're at.

Cultivate empathy

Drawing the Devil card to represent your partner doesn't mean they're wrong, instead it indicates the kind of experience they're having - one where maybe they feel trapped in a mess they can't solve. That context is important when you draw a card about the care they need from you.

Similarly, drawing the Six of Swords for yourself might remind you that you're going through a long transition, and you need your partner with you on the journey. Being able to provide this background when asking your partner for the care you need during this transition is likely to make the request go more smoothly

Move forward together

While the earlier cards focused on your individual needs and tasks, the final card brings you and your partner together - it transforms you from being each other's responsibility into a united team. The Two of Cups here could indicate a return to romance that's been lacking, while the Judgement card may indicate that it's time to deal with past issues - and that professional support could help.

1. Me

2. My partner

3. The care I need from my partner

4. The care my partner needs from me

5. The care we need to give our relationship

FAMILY

The relationship between family and care is a complex one. The ways in which care was and wasn't shown and felt in your family when you were young will likely have had a profound effect on your relationship with care – how you receive it, how you give it, and how you prioritize it for yourself.

Illuminate your care history

The cards you pull for this spread can help you look at your relationship with care through fresh eyes. By drawing cards to illuminate what care looked like when you first learned what care even was, you'll be able to gain a better understanding of how you give and receive care in your life. You'll also better understand what you can do to be a better caregiver and recipient of care in the family relationships that matter to you now.

Allow for surprise

The spread plays out across three columns. In the first column, you'll draw cards relating to your history with care, particularly how it functioned in your family relationships in the past, and how you were affected by the quality of care you received. You may find that the cards you pull are surprisingly more negative or more positive than you might have anticipated - lean into that, and dig deep into how the cards you draw can help you reconsider and reframe your past.

Journal your feelings

You might want to do some deeper journaling to explore what you see here before moving on to the second and third columns. Ask yourself these follow-up questions while considering your first two cards:

- *What do these cards show me about what care meant to me as a child?*
- *How do these spreads mirror the kind of care I value now?*
- *What do I wish was different about my family's approach to care?*
- *What kind of care am I glad I learned from my family?*

Apply care lessons

In the second and third columns, you'll build on what the first two cards indicated about the kind of care you learned from your family. You've now got the chance to apply this insight to the care they need from you now, and most importantly, how you can ask for and give that much needed care. From the third card position onwards, think about how the cards relate to whoever it is you consider family today.

1. How care has functioned in my family relationships in the past
2. How that quality of care affected me
3. The care I need from my family now
4. How I can ask for that care
5. The care my family needs from me
6. How I can give that care

CONFLICT

This is a spread about taking care through conflict – not 'taking care' in the sense of making it go away or solving it as a problem, but instead tending to the wound at the centre of the conflict, and caring for yourself while you navigate the issue you're facing.

Tend to your wounds

If you're using this spread to work through a conflict at your job, drawing the Three of Pentacles or Five of Wands might tell you that you're dealing with a 'too many cooks' situation - that the conflict is really rooted in the fact that more than one person (yourself included) feels entitled to the driver's seat when it comes to solving a problem. It hints that the clash is about each person's need to prove themselves useful, expert, and capable.

Take time to cool off

The second card in this spread gives you guidance about how you can tend to the conflict by providing care to the issue to help soothe it. The Eight of Cups here probably means that the best care you can offer is a retreat - give things time to cool off, or even recognize that the kindest thing you can do is give up your claim to being right in the conflict and move on. The Four of Swords advises rest for all involved before working together toward a solution.

See where care is needed

The final two cards deal directly with you - how you see and care for yourself amidst the conflict.

It's not possible to provide care if we can't see where care is needed; that's why it's so important to identify our own role in the conflict we're trying to take care of. The Ten of Wands here could be a sign that you've brought too much of your own stuff to the table, and that your feelings, desires, and beliefs about the issue are blinding you and perpetuating the conflict. The Three of Swords could be about how you might be letting painful experiences from the past colour the issue now at hand.

Face yourself

Acknowledging your own role in a conflict is essential but difficult work, so the final card is a reminder to prioritize care in this process. Whatever card you draw here will offer sound advice on how you can tend to yourself and take steps to move toward a resolution.

1. The root of the conflict

2. How a sense of care can help smooth the conflict

3. My role in the conflict

4. The self-care I need to move past the conflict

CHOICE

The choice spreads in this book so far have been designed to help you evaluate your options and make the choice that's best for you. But this spread is a little different – not only because it shifts the focus away from the act of choosing, but also because you will probably notice it's only made up of one card.

Choose care

We all make choices all day long. We choose what to eat, what to wear, whether or not we need an umbrella, if we should start our morning by opening our phone or meditating or making our bed or journaling or exercising or going back to bed. We choose to choose, or we choose to avoid choosing.

What we rarely choose is to prioritize our care while we move through our lives making myriad choices. Instinct and logic tend to be the key drivers of our choices - we choose because something feels right, or because it makes logical sense. But with this spread, I want you to set aside instinct and logic and consider how your choices impact the quality of care you are able to give and receive.

Cultivate quality care

How, this spread can help you ask yourself, can your choices result in a better quality of care for yourself, the people you love, the environment you live in? Drawing a card for this one card spread is simple, but the revelations you get may surprise you.

When you're faced with a choice - even something as simple as what to eat for breakfast - this spread can help you remember to make choices based on care. Temperance could remind you to fuel and hydrate your body for the day ahead. The Three of Cups could prompt you to reach out to friends for an impromptu coffee date, because surrounding yourself with people you love is the best way to care for yourself right now. The Three of Swords, on the other hand, might be a prompt for comfort food - you're in the midst of something hard, and you deserve to make yourself feel safe.

Nourish yourself

Using this spread daily can help you make choices that nourish you instead of drain you. When you choose to prioritize care in your life, your approach to choice will change, the way you set boundaries and build bridges will change, the quality of care you give to yourself and others will change, and your sense of safety and peace will grow.

1

1. How I can choose to prioritize care right now

CARE

CONFIDENCE

This spread is all about acknowledging and appreciating the ways that different modes of care impact your confidence. It's a chance to stand back and see how putting an emphasis on care helps you grow into yourself; how care strengthens you and expands your horizons.

Reflect on positive care

Before you begin, I want you to take a few minutes to meditate or journal on some of your past positive experiences with care. Ask yourself:

- *Who in my life gives me care in a way that makes me feel empowered?*
- *What kind of care do I most enjoy giving to others?*
- *When have I asked for the care I needed and got it?*
- *When have I taken a risk by offering care, and learned from it?*

Seek out connections

With the answers to those questions in mind, shuffle your deck and lay all three cards out at once. Look first for connecting visual motifs across the cards – does anything jump out? Visual patterns may tell you a lot about how the theme of care plays out in your life, so take note. For example, if you notice a recurring visual motif of butterflies in the cards, you have the opportunity to reflect on the transformative power of care, and how that's manifested in your own life.

Care for your confidence

Once you've looked at the big picture, dig in to explore each card on its own. Each card is related back to a specific pillar of care, and how that kind of care helps you grow confidence. The first card asks you to investigate how self-care gives you confidence, so make a note of how this relates to your self-care practices, or if it inspires ideas for new practices to grow confidence.

Accept and give care confidently

The second card looks at how being cared for helps you grow your confidence. When you look at this card, think back to how it could relate to the memories you journaled and meditated on before starting this spread. Think too about how you could accept more of this kind of care into your life. The final card will help you see how giving care grows your confidence. Think of this card as a call to action: by going out into the world and offering care, you'll build your confidence, but because you know that receiving care is also a confidence builder, you'll probably help someone else grow theirs too.

1. How self-care impacts my confidence
2. How being cared for by others impacts my confidence
3. How caring for others/my environment impacts my confidence

Cycle of Care

In his cult classic book, *Zen and the Art of Motorcycle Maintenance*, Robert M. Pirsig makes a sharp observation about the relationship between care and quality. He says: 'Care and quality are internal and external aspects of the same thing. A person who sees quality and feels it as he works is a person who cares. A person who cares about what he sees and does is a person who's bound to have some characteristic of quality'.

Put another way: the act of care allows you to live a quality life – whatever that means to you. Pirsig's words suggest that when we're aware of what quality means to us, we're more inclined toward the act of care. It's a brilliant way to think about all kinds of care. The care we give to others, ourselves, our things, our lives, as well as the care we receive, all offer lessons about what we value, all offer us the chance to reflect on what it means to live a quality life, and the role that care plays in that life.

It raises important questions like: If care is the act through which you bestow quality, what kind of care means the most to you? And how can understanding the quality that others value help you care meaningfully for the people in your life?

Ultimately, exploring the relationship between what quality and care mean for you brings us full circle back to Plato, whose words guided us into this season. When you know yourself, you can better care for yourself.

When you mash up Plato's idea of care with Robert M. Pirsig's, what you get is the essential idea that the more you know about yourself and others, the more meaningful the care you give yourself and others can be.

Journal prompts

Take some time to reflect back on what Plato and Pirsig have to say about care. Explore the ways in which knowing your own definition of quality – and the definition of quality held by those you care for – facilitates more meaningful! care.

Ask yourself:

- *What is my vision for a quality life?*
- *How can the act of care help me attain that quality life?*
- *Do I understand what a quality life looks like for the people I love and care for?*
- *How can I apply care that helps my loved ones raise the quality of their own lives?*

TAROT MANTRAS FOR CARE

As this season winds down, I want you to think about how you can distil the most powerful takeaways from your Season of Care into a mantra that you can carry with you long after you close this book. Use the tarot cards which have affected you most deeply over the season – or look back to the Star, the Empress, or Strength to inspire you.

If you're not sure what your mantra could be, feel free to take one of mine:

A care mantra inspired by the Star

I know that caring for others demands that I care for myself first. I embrace meaningful acts of self-care because not only do I deserve to care for myself, but the people in my life deserve the best, most well-cared for version of me.

A care mantra inspired by Strength

I am strong enough to care for myself, my loved ones, my environment, and my community. I respect the hell out of myself for prioritizing the hard work of care in a world that would have me gloss over it.

A care mantra inspired by the Empress:

I am committed to cultivating an environment of care for everyone in my life – myself included.

Think about how you can bring your mantra into your personal self-care practices. If self-care looks like time in the yoga studio for you, can you meditate on your mantra during sessions? If self-care for you is journaling, can you write your mantra out at the top or bottom of a page? If self-care is a hot shower or a movie night or a massage, repeat the mantra before you start and when you finish.

Refer back to your mantra whenever you feel stuck, or whenever you want to remind yourself that care is your birth right.

REFLECTIONS

Your Season of Care has reached its end, and it's time to prepare to move forward. But before you do, use this spread to meditate on your deepening relationship to care, and everything you've learned this season.

Uncover your experience

You'll know best how your relationship with care has evolved over the past few months, but drawing cards will help you uncover surprising aspects of your experience that may have otherwise gone unnoticed and uncelebrated. I really believe that's what the cards do best – they help us expand our knowledge by offering us different vantage points to our experiences.

Digest the message

To get the most out of this spread, draw each card one by one, and give yourself ample time to digest what each card can reveal about your journey through the Season of Care. You may even want to take a minute, before drawing a card, to journal through the spread prompt, so that when you draw each card, you have some context to work with.

Cherish your experiences

However you choose to use this reflection spread, the important thing is that you do reflect. Reflection, in itself, is a vital act of care. It's a gift you give yourself – the opportunity to sit with your experiences, cherish them, commit them to memory, and allow them to nourish you as you move forward.

Take care

You've spent the past year reflecting, caring for yourself by taking time, space, and energy to work through the 52 tarot spreads in this book. I hope as this season, and this book, come to a close, that you feel richer for the moments spent communing with yourself, and that you're empowered to care for yourself through another year of growth, shadow, and change.

1. How I cared for myself this season
2. How I cared for others this season
3. What I learned about care this season

About the Author

Chelsey Pippin Mizzi is a writer, tarot reader, and the founder of Pip Cards Tarot, a tarot consultancy helping creatives unblock, generate new ideas, and connect to their inner artist through tarot. Her writing has been featured in *BuzzFeed*, *New York Magazine's The Strategist*, *Metro*, and other titles. She was born and raised in the United States, and has lived in Iceland, Turkey, and England. Today, she lives in France with her partner, dog, and cat. *The Tarot Spreads Yearbook* is her first book.

Follow Chelsey on Instagram, TikTok, and Twitter at @pipcardstarot, or book a reading directly at pipcardstarot.com.

Acknowledgements

Thank you to Zacharie Mizzi, my favourite person in the universe, for everything and more – I love you. To my family: Mom, Dad, Cloe, Brady, my wonderful Namaw, Grandma, Granny, both my Grandpas, my aunts, uncles, and cousins. Thank you to the Mizzis et al: Arielle, Michel, Raph, Lison, Octave, Marie, Polo, Thomas, Mathilde. Thank you to my friends: Katherine Dunn, Sara Gray, Laura Kemp, Laura Jones, Nick Wells, Carrie Ellis, Katie Crosta, and many others.

Thank you Ailbhe Malone, for giving me my first real writing job and starting my career. Thank you Katy Hristova and Hayley King, the best beta readers and excellent friends. Thank you London Writers Salon, especially Lindsey Trout Hughes and Lauren McMenemy. Thank you to my wider writing community – I'm lucky to get to write alongside so many brilliant, kind people.

Thank you to Maddy Belton, Jane Graham-Maw and the whole team at the Graham-Maw Christie Agency for taking such good care of me. Thank you to Lizzie Kaye and everyone at David & Charles for your faith in me and your beautiful vision for this book. Thanks to Cara, for spoiling me with such gorgeous illustrations. Thanks also to Kate Bliss, Gina Felsted, Maria Kekki, Clare Laizens, Morgan Thomas, Vix Maxwell, Nix at Seedling Spiritual, and many others for all kinds of help and support.

And finally, to my clients – helping you connect and understand yourselves through tarot is the joy of my life, thank you for trusting me to read for you.

Index

Aces 30, 36, 43, 107
action 20, 90, 114
astrology 13

balance 52
burn-out 122

Care 50
    Cycle of 138–9
    Season of 7, 9, 110–41
careers 9, 26–7, 58–9, 90–1, 122–3
Change 26
    Cycle of 106–7
    Season of 7, 78–109
choice 9, 38–9, 70–1, 102–3, 134–5
confidence 9, 40–1, 72–3, 104–5,
    136–7
conflict 9, 36–7, 68–9, 100–1, 132–3
court cards 11
    see also specific cards
Cups 10, 32, 102, 112–13, 124
    Ace of 30
    Eight of 30, 90, 132
    Five of 32
    Four of 32
    King of 112
    Page of 28
    Queen of 112, 116
    Six of 40, 104, 112
    Three of 116, 134
    Two of 32, 126, 128

Death 30, 80, 107, 108
defining tarot 6
Devil 36, 48, 75, 80, 104, 128

elements 13, 16
Empress 16–17, 43, 58, 113, 139

family 9, 34–5, 66–7, 98–9, 130–1
Fool 12–13, 118
Fool's Journey, The 10, 80
friendship 9, 30–1, 56, 62–3, 94–5,
    126–7
future, the 11, 12

greed 52–3
Growth 104, 15
    Cycle of 42–3
    Season of 7, 14–45, 112

Hanged One 28, 118
help, asking for 120
Hermit 30, 126
High Priestess 48, 75
hobbies 124

intentions 18–19, 50–1, 82–3, 114–15
intimacy 32

journaling 8, 12, 42, 54, 74, 76, 82, 96,
    106, 130, 136, 138
Judgement 49, 75, 128
Jung, Carl 47

learning types 24
Lovers 52, 66, 94

Magician 124
Major Arcana 10, 48, 80, 102, 112, 124
    see also specific cards
manifestation 20
mantras 43, 75, 107, 139
meaning-making 6
mind 9, 24–5, 56–7, 88–9, 120–1
Minor Arcana 10
    see also Cups; Pentacles;
    Swords; Wands
Moon 48, 75

Nin, Anaïs 42

past, the 11, 12, 90
Pentacles 10, 16–17, 40, 43, 84, 112,
    124, 26
    Ace of 36, 43
    Eight of 17, 43, 107, 112
    Five of 43, 66, 70
    Four of 112
    King of 24, 122
    Knight of 12–13
    Page of 104
    Queen of 16–17
    Seven of 16, 112
    Six of 52
    Three of 26, 96, 126, 132
    Two of 26
Pirsig, Robert M. 138
Plato 111, 138
play 9, 28–9, 60–1, 92–3, 124–5
present, the 11, 12

readings, sample 12–13
reflections 44–5, 76–7, 108–9, 140–1
resources 9, 20–1, 52–3, 84–5, 116–17
romance 9, 32–3, 64–5, 96–7, 128–9

self-love 32
Shadow
    connection with your 54
    Cycle of 74–5
    Season of 7, 9, 46–77
soul, growth 15
Soul Seasons 7
    see also Care, Season of;
    Change, Season of; Growth,
    Season of; Shadow, Season of
spirit 9, 22–3, 54–5, 86–7, 118–19
spreads 8–9, 11–13
    Care 114–37, 140–1
    Change 82–105, 108–9
    Growth 18–41, 44–5
    Shadow 50–73, 76–7
Star 40, 52, 64, 112–13, 124, 139
Strength 113, 139
Sun 49
Swords 10, 49, 84, 112, 124
    Eight of 30, 94
    Five of 58
    Four of 52, 64, 112, 132
    Nine of 30
    Seven of 104
    Six of 30, 112, 128
    Ten of 72, 112, 116
    Three of 24, 66, 112, 132, 134
    Two of 38

Temperance 58, 80, 82, 134
Tower 48, 80–2, 107–8, 126

Wands 10, 32, 112, 124
    Eight of 12–13
    Five of 32, 132
    Four of 32, 66, 72, 112
    Nine of 32, 100, 112, 116
    Page of 28
    Queen of 122
    Seven of 90
    Ten of 112, 132
    Three of 112
    Two of 112
work-life balance 58

This book has been printed on paper from
approved suppliers and made from pulp from
sustainable sources.

MIX
Paper from
responsible sources
FSC® C012521

Printed in China through Asia Pacific Offset Ltd for:
David and Charles, Ltd
Suite A, Tourism House, Pynes Hill, Exeter, EX2 5WS

10 9 8 7 6 5 4 3 2 1

Publishing Director: Ame Verso
Senior Commissioning Editor: Lizzie Kaye
Managing Editor: Jeni Chown
Editor: Jessica Cropper
Copy Editors: Jane Trollope and Clare Ashton
Head of Design: Anna Wade
Designers: Lucy Ridley and Jo Langdon
Pre-press Designer: Ali Stark
Illustrations: Cara Hudson
Production Manager: Beverley Richardson

David and Charles publishes high-quality books on
a wide range of subjects. For more information visit
www.davidandcharles.com.

Share your stories with us on social media using
#dandcbooks and follow us on Facebook and
Instagram by searching for @dandcbooks.

Layout of the digital edition of this book may vary
depending on reader hardware and display settings.